Programming PyTorch for Deep Learning

Creating and Deploying Deep Learning Applications

Ian Pointer

Beijing · Boston · Farnham · Sebastopol · Tokyo

Programming PyTorch for Deep Learning

by Ian Pointer

Published by O'Reilly Media, Inc., 1005 Gravenstein Highway North, Sebastopol, CA 95472.

O'Reilly books may be purchased for educational, business, or sales promotional use. Online editions are also available for most titles (*http://oreilly.com*). For more information, contact our corporate/institutional sales department: 800-998-9938 or *corporate@oreilly.com*.

Development Editor: Melissa Potter	**Indexer:** WordCo Indexing Services, Inc.
Acquisitions Editor: Jonathan Hassell	**Interior Designer:** David Futato
Production Editor: Katherine Tozer	**Cover Designer:** Susan Thompson
Copyeditor: Sharon Wilkey	**Illustrator:** Rebecca Demarest
Proofreader: Christina Edwards	

September 2019:   First Edition

Revision History for the First Edition
2019-09-20:   First Release

See *http://oreilly.com/catalog/errata.csp?isbn=9781492045359* for release details.

The O'Reilly logo is a registered trademark of O'Reilly Media, Inc. *Programming PyTorch for Deep Learning*, the cover image, and related trade dress are trademarks of O'Reilly Media, Inc.

978-1-492-04535-9

[LSI]

Table of Contents

Preface

Deep Learning in the World Today

Hello and welcome! This book will introduce you to deep learning via PyTorch, an open source library released by Facebook in 2017. Unless you've had your head stuck in the ground in a very good impression of an ostrich the past few years, you can't have helped but notice that neural networks are everywhere these days. They've gone from being the *really cool bit of computer science that people learn about and then do nothing with* to being carried around with us in our phones every day to improve our pictures or listen to our voice commands. Our email software reads our email and produces context-sensitive replies, our speakers listen out for us, cars drive by themselves, and the computer has finally bested humans at Go. We're also seeing the technology being used for more nefarious ends in authoritarian countries, where neural network–backed sentinels can pick faces out of crowds and make a decision on whether they should be apprehended.

And yet, despite the feeling that this has all happened so fast, the concepts of neural networks and deep learning go back a long way. The proof that such a network could function as a way of replacing *any* mathematical function in an approximate way, which underpins the idea that neural networks can be trained for many different tasks, dates back to 1989,[1] and convolutional neural networks were being used to recognize digits on check in the late '90s. There's been a solid foundation building up all this time, so why does it feel like an explosion occurred in the last 10 years?

There are many reasons, but prime among them has to be the surge in *graphical processing units* (GPUs) performance and their increasing affordability. Designed originally for gaming, GPUs need to perform countless millions of matrix operations per second in order to render all the polygons for the driving or shooting game you're

---

[1] See "Approximation by Superpositions of Sigmoidal Functions" (*https://oreil.ly/BQ8-9*), by George Cybenko (1989).

playing on your console or PC, operations that a standard CPU just isn't optimized for. A 2009 paper, "Large-Scale Deep Unsupervised Learning Using Graphics Processors" by Rajat Raina et al., pointed out that training neural networks was also based on performing lots of matrix operations, and so these add-on graphics cards could be used to speed up training as well as make larger, *deeper* neural network architectures feasible for the first time. Other important techniques such as *Dropout* (which we will look at in Chapter 3) were also introduced in the last decade as ways to not just speed up training but make training more *generalized* (so that the network doesn't just learn to recognize the training data, a problem called *overfitting* that we'll encounter in the next chapter). In the last couple of years, companies have taken this GPU-based approach to the next level, with Google creating what it describes as *tensor processing units* (TPUs), which are devices custom-built for performing deep learning as fast as possible, and are even available to the general public as part of their Google Cloud ecosystem.

Another way to chart deep learning's progress over the past decade is through the ImageNet competition. A massive database of over 14 million pictures, manually labeled into 20,000 categories, ImageNet is a treasure trove of labeled data for machine learning purposes. Since 2010, the yearly ImageNet Large Scale Visual Recognition Challenge has sought to test all comers against a 1,000-category subset of the database, and until 2012, error rates for tackling the challenge rested around 25%. That year, however, a deep convolutional neural network won the competition with an error of 16%, massively outperforming all other entrants. In the years that followed, that error rate got pushed down further and further, to the point that in 2015, the ResNet architecture obtained a result of 3.6%, which beat the average human performance on ImageNet (5%). We had been outclassed.

But What Is Deep Learning Exactly, and Do I Need a PhD to Understand It?

Deep learning's definition often is more confusing than enlightening. A way of defining it is to say that deep learning is a machine learning technique that uses multiple and numerous layers of nonlinear transforms to progressively extract features from raw input. Which is true, but it doesn't really help, does it? I prefer to describe it as a technique to solve problems by providing the inputs and desired outputs and letting the computer find the solution, normally using a neural network.

One thing about deep learning that scares off a lot of people is the mathematics. Look at just about any paper in the field and you'll be subjected to almost impenetrable amounts of notation with Greek letters all over the place, and you'll likely run screaming for the hills. Here's the thing: for the most part, you don't need to be a math genius to use deep learning techniques. In fact, for most day-to-day basic uses of the technology, you don't need to know much at all, and to really understand what's going on (as you'll see in Chapter 2), you only have to stretch a little to understand concepts that you probably learned in high school. So don't be too scared about the math. By the end of Chapter 3, you'll be able to put together an image classifier that rivals what the best minds in 2015 could offer with just a few lines of code.

PyTorch

As I mentioned back at the start, PyTorch is an open source offering from Facebook that facilitates writing deep learning code in Python. It has two lineages. First, and perhaps not entirely surprisingly given its name, it derives many features and concepts from Torch, which was a Lua-based neural network library that dates back to 2002. Its other major parent is Chainer, created in Japan in 2015. Chainer was one of the first neural network libraries to offer an eager approach to differentiation instead of defining static graphs, allowing for greater flexibility in the way networks are created, trained, and operated. The combination of the Torch legacy plus the ideas from Chainer has made PyTorch popular over the past couple of years.[2]

The library also comes with modules that help with manipulating text, images, and audio (torchtext, torchvision, and torchaudio), along with built-in variants of popular architectures such as ResNet (with weights that can be downloaded to provide assistance with techniques like *transfer learning,* which you'll see in Chapter 4).

Aside from Facebook, PyTorch has seen quick acceptance by industry, with companies such as Twitter, Salesforce, Uber, and NVIDIA using it in various ways for their deep learning work. Ah, but I sense a question coming....

What About TensorFlow?

Yes, let's address the rather large, Google-branded elephant in the corner. What does PyTorch offer that TensorFlow doesn't? Why should you learn PyTorch instead?

The answer is that traditional TensorFlow works in a different way than PyTorch that has major implications for code and debugging. In TensorFlow, you use the library to build up a graph representation of the neural network architecture and then you execute operations on that graph, which happens within the TensorFlow library. This method of declarative programming is somewhat at odds with Python's more imperative paradigm, meaning that Python TensorFlow programs can look and feel somewhat odd and difficult to understand. The other issue is that the static graph declaration can make dynamically altering the architecture during training and inference time a lot more complicated and stuffed with boilerplate than with PyTorch's approach.

---

2 Note that PyTorch borrows ideas from Chainer, but not actual code.

For these reasons, PyTorch has become popular in research-oriented communities. The number of papers submitted to the International Conference on Learning Representations that mention *PyTorch* has jumped 200% in the past year, and the number of papers mentioning *TensorFlow* has increased almost equally. PyTorch is definitely here to stay.

However, things are changing in more recent versions of TensorFlow. A new feature called *eager execution* has been recently added to the library that allows it to work similarly to PyTorch and will be the paradigm promoted in TensorFlow 2.0. But as it's new resources outside of Google that help you learn this new method of working with TensorFlow are thin on the ground, plus you'd need years of work out there to understand the other paradigm in order to get the most out of the library.

But none of this should make you think poorly of TensorFlow; it remains an industry-proven library with support from one of the biggest companies on the planet. PyTorch (backed, of course, by a different biggest company on the planet) is, I would say, a more streamlined and focused approach to deep learning and differential programming. Because it doesn't have to continue supporting older, crustier APIs, it is easier to teach and become productive in PyTorch than in TensorFlow.

Where does Keras fit in with this? So many good questions! Keras is a high-level deep learning library that originally supported Theano and TensorFlow, and now also supports certain other frames such as Apache MXNet. It provides certain features such as training, validation, and test loops that the lower-level frameworks leave as an exercise for the developer, as well as simple methods of building up neural network architectures. It has contributed hugely to the take-up of TensorFlow, and is now part of TensorFlow itself (as `tf.keras`) as well as continuing to be a separate project. PyTorch, in comparison, is something of a middle ground between the low level of raw TensorFlow and Keras; we will have to write our own training and inference routines, but creating neural networks is almost as straightforward (and I would say that PyTorch's approach to making and reusing architectures is much more logical to a Python developer than some of Keras's magic).

As you'll see in this book, although PyTorch is common in more research-oriented positions, with the advent of PyTorch 1.0, it's perfectly suited to production use cases.

Conventions Used in This Book

The following typographical conventions are used in this book:

Italic
> Indicates new terms, URLs, email addresses, filenames, and file extensions.

`Constant width`
> Used for program listings, as well as within paragraphs to refer to program elements such as variable or function names, databases, data types, environment variables, statements, and keywords.

`Constant width bold`
> Shows commands or other text that should be typed literally by the user.

`Constant width italic`
> Shows text that should be replaced with user-supplied values or by values determined by context.

> This element signifies a tip or suggestion.

> This element signifies a general note.

> This element indicates a warning or caution.

Using Code Examples

Supplemental material (including code examples and exercises) is available for download at *https://oreil.ly/pytorch-github*.

This book is here to help you get your job done. In general, if example code is offered with this book, you may use it in your programs and documentation. You do not need to contact us for permission unless you're reproducing a significant portion of the code. For example, writing a program that uses several chunks of code from this book does not require permission. Selling or distributing a CD-ROM of examples from O'Reilly books does require permission. Answering a question by citing this book and quoting example code does not require permission. Incorporating a significant amount of example code from this book into your product's documentation does require permission.

We appreciate, but do not require, attribution. An attribution usually includes the title, author, publisher, and ISBN. For example: "*Programming PyTorch for Deep Learning* by Ian Pointer (O'Reilly). Copyright 2019 Ian Pointer, 978-1-492-04535-9."

If you feel your use of code examples falls outside fair use or the permission given above, feel free to contact us at *permissions@oreilly.com*.

O'Reilly Online Learning

 For almost 40 years, *O'Reilly Media* has provided technology and business training, knowledge, and insight to help companies succeed.

Our unique network of experts and innovators share their knowledge and expertise through books, articles, conferences, and our online learning platform. O'Reilly's online learning platform gives you on-demand access to live training courses, in-depth learning paths, interactive coding environments, and a vast collection of text and video from O'Reilly and 200+ other publishers. For more information, please visit *http://oreilly.com*.

How to Contact Us

Please address comments and questions concerning this book to the publisher:

O'Reilly Media, Inc.
1005 Gravenstein Highway North
Sebastopol, CA 95472
800-998-9938 (in the United States or Canada)
707-829-0515 (international or local)
707-829-0104 (fax)

We have a web page for this book, where we list errata, examples, and any additional information. You can access this page at *https://oreil.ly/prgrming-pytorch-for-dl*.

Email *bookquestions@oreilly.com* to comment or ask technical questions about this book.

For more information about our books, courses, conferences, and news, see our website at *http://www.oreilly.com*.

Find us on Facebook: *http://facebook.com/oreilly*

Follow us on Twitter: *http://twitter.com/oreillymedia*

Watch us on YouTube: *http://www.youtube.com/oreillymedia*

Acknowledgments

A big thank you to my editor, Melissa Potter, my family, and Tammy Edlund for all their help in making this book possible. Thank you, also, to the technical reviewers who provided valuable feedback throughout the writing process, including Phil Rhodes, David Mertz, Charles Givre, Dominic Monn, Ankur Patel, and Sarah Nagy.

CHAPTER 1

Getting Started with PyTorch

In this chapter we set up all we need for working with PyTorch. Once we've done that, every chapter following will build on this initial foundation, so it's important that we get it right. This leads to our first fundamental question: should you build a custom deep learning computer or just use one of the many cloud-based resources available?

Building a Custom Deep Learning Machine

There is an urge when diving into deep learning to build yourself a monster for all your compute needs. You can spend days looking over different types of graphics cards, learning the memory lanes possible CPU selections will offer you, the best sort of memory to buy, and just how big an SSD drive you can purchase to make your disk access as fast as possible. I am not claiming any immunity from this; I spent a month a couple of years ago making a list of parts and building a new computer on my dining room table.

My advice, especially if you're new to deep learning, is this: don't do it. You can easily spend several thousands of dollars on a machine that you may not use all that much. Instead, I recommend that you work through this book by using cloud resources (in either Amazon Web Services, Google Cloud, or Microsoft Azure) and only then start thinking about building your own machine if you feel that you require a single machine for 24/7 operation. You *do not* need to make a massive investment in hardware to run any of the code in this book.

You might not ever need to build a custom machine for yourself. There's something of a sweet spot, where it can be cheaper to build a custom rig if you know your calculations are always going to be restricted to a single machine (with at most a handful of GPUs). However, if your compute starts to require spanning multiple machines and

GPUs, the cloud becomes appealing again. Given the cost of putting a custom machine together, I'd think long and hard before diving in.

If I haven't managed to put you off from building your own, the following sections provide suggestions for what you would need to do so.

GPU

The heart of every deep learning box, the GPU, is what is going to power the majority of PyTorch's calculations, and it's likely going to be the most expensive component in your machine. In recent years, the prices of GPUs have increased, and the supplies have dwindled, because of their use in mining cryptocurrency like Bitcoin. Thankfully, that bubble seems to be receding, and supplies of GPUs are back to being a little more plentiful.

At the time of this writing, I recommend obtaining the NVIDIA GeForce RTX 2080 Ti. For a cheaper option, feel free to go for the 1080 Ti (though if you are weighing the decision to get the 1080 Ti for budgetary reasons, I again suggest that you look at cloud options instead). Although AMD-manufactured GPU cards do exist, their support in PyTorch is currently not good enough to recommend anything other than an NVIDIA card. But keep a lookout for their ROCm technology, which should eventually make them a credible alternative in the GPU space.

CPU/Motherboard

You'll probably want to spring for a Z370 series motherboard. Many people will tell you that the CPU doesn't matter for deep learning and that you can get by with a lower-speed CPU as long as you have a powerful GPU. In my experience, you'll be surprised at how often the CPU can become a bottleneck, especially when working with augmented data.

RAM

More RAM is good, as it means you can keep more data inside without having to hit the much slower disk storage (especially important during your training stages). You should be looking at a minimum of 64GB DDR4 memory for your machine.

Storage

Storage for a custom rig should be installed in two classes: first, an M2-interface solid-state drive (SSD)—as big as you can afford—for your *hot* data to keep access as fast as possible when you're actively working on a project. For the second class of storage, add in a 4TB Serial ATA (SATA) drive for data that you're not actively working on, and transfer to *hot* and *cold* storage as required.

I recommend that you take a look at PCPartPicker (*https://pcpartpicker.com*) to glance at other people's deep learning machines (you can see all the weird and wild case ideas, too!). You'll get a feel for lists of machine parts and associated prices, which can fluctuate wildly, especially for GPU cards.

Now that you've looked at your local, physical machine options, it's time to head to the clouds.

Deep Learning in the Cloud

OK, so why is the cloud option better, you might ask? Especially if you've looked at the Amazon Web Services (AWS) pricing scheme and worked out that building a deep learning machine will pay for itself within six months? Think about it: if you're just starting out, you are not going to be using that machine 24/7 for those six months. You're just not. Which means that you can shut off the cloud machine and pay pennies for the data being stored in the meantime.

And if you're starting out, you don't need to go all out and use one of NVIDIA's leviathan Tesla V100 cards attached to your cloud instance straightaway. You can start out with one of the much cheaper (sometimes even free) K80-based instances and move up to the more powerful card when you're ready. That is a trifle less expensive than buying a basic GPU card and upgrading to a 2080Ti on your custom box. Plus if you want to add eight V100 cards to a single instance, you can do it with just a few clicks. Try doing that with your own hardware.

The other issue is maintenance. If you get yourself into the good habit of re-creating your cloud instances on a regular basis (ideally starting anew every time you come back to work on your experiments), you'll almost always have a machine that is up to date. If you have your own machine, updating is up to you. This is where I confess that I do have my own custom deep learning machine, and I ignored the Ubuntu installation on it for so long that it fell out of supported updates, resulting in an eventual day spent trying to get the system back to a place where it was receiving updates again. Embarrassing.

Anyway, you've made the decision to go to the cloud. Hurrah! Next: which provider?

Google Colaboratory

But wait—before we look at providers, what if you don't want to do any work at all? None of that pesky building a machine or having to go through all the trouble of setting up instances in the cloud? Where's the really lazy option? Google has the right thing for you. *Colaboratory* (or *Colab*) (*https://colab.research.google.com*) is a mostly free, zero-installation-required custom Jupyter Notebook environment. You'll need a Google account to set up your own notebooks. Figure 1-1 shows a screenshot of a notebook created in Colab.

What makes Colab a great way to dive into deep learning is that it includes preinstalled versions of TensorFlow and PyTorch, so you don't have to do any setup beyond typing `import torch`, and every user can get free access to a NVIDIA T4 GPU for up to 12 hours of continuous runtime. For free. To put that in context, empirical research suggests that you get about half the speed of a 1080 Ti for training, but with an extra 5GB of memory so you can store larger models. It also offers the ability to connect to more recent GPUs and Google's custom TPU hardware in a paid option, but you can pretty much do every example in this book for nothing with Colab. For that reason, I recommend using Colab alongside this book to begin with, and then you can decide to branch out to dedicated cloud instances and/or your own personal deep learning server if needed.

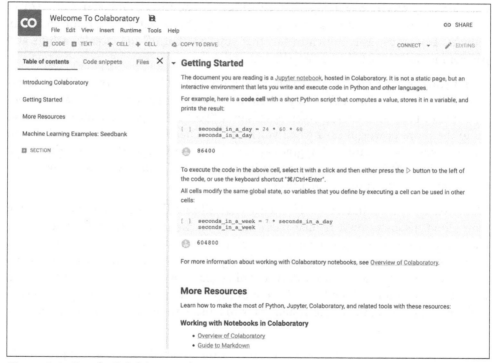

Figure 1-1. Google Colab(oratory)

Colab is the zero-effort approach, but you may want to have a little more control over how things are installed or get Secure Shell (SSH) access to your instance on the cloud, so let's have a look at what the main cloud providers offer.

Cloud Providers

Each of the big three cloud providers (Amazon Web Services, Google Cloud Platform, and Microsoft's Azure) offers GPU-based instances (also referred to as *virtual machines* or *VMs*) and official images to deploy on those instances. They have all you need to get up and running without having to install drivers and Python libraries yourself. Let's have a run-through of what each provider offers.

Amazon Web Services

AWS, the 800-pound gorilla of the cloud market, is more than happy to fulfill your GPU needs and offers the P2 and P3 instance types to help you out. (The G3 instance type tends to be used more in actual graphics-based applications like video encoding, so we won't cover it here.) The P2 instances use the older NVIDIA K80 cards (a maximum of 16 can be connected to one instance), and the P3 instances use the blazing-fast NVIDIA V100 cards (and you can strap eight of those onto one instance if you dare).

If you're going to use AWS, my recommendation for this book is to go with the p2.xlarge class. This will cost you just 90 cents an hour at the time of this writing and provides plenty of power for working through the examples. You may want to bump up to the P3 classes when you start working on some meaty Kaggle competitions.

Creating a running deep learning box on AWS is incredibly easy:

1. Sign into the AWS console.
2. Select EC2 and click Launch Instance.
3. Search for the Deep Learning AMI (Ubuntu) option and select it.
4. Choose p2.xlarge as your instance type.
5. Launch the instance, either by creating a new key pair or reusing an existing key pair.
6. Connect to the instance by using SSH and redirecting port 8888 on your local machine to the instance:

   ```
   ssh -L localhost:8888:localhost:8888 \
   -i your .pem filename ubuntu@your instance DNS
   ```

7. Start Jupyter Notebook by entering **jupyter notebook**. Copy the URL that gets generated and paste it into your browser to access Jupyter.

Remember to shut down your instance when you're not using it! You can do this by right-clicking the instance in the web interface and selecting the Shutdown option. This will shut down the instance, and you won't be charged for the instance while it's not running. However, you *will* be charged for the storage space that you have allocated for it even if the instance is turned off, so be aware of that. To delete the instance and storage entirely, select the Terminate option instead.

Azure

Like AWS, Azure offers a mixture of cheaper K80-based instances and more expensive Tesla V100 instances. Azure also offers instances based on the older P100 hardware as a halfway point between the other two. Again, I recommend the instance type that uses a single K80 (NC6) for this book, which also costs 90 cents per hour, and move onto other NC, NCv2 (P100), or NCv3 (V100) types as you need them.

Here's how you set up the VM in Azure:

1. Log in to the Azure portal and find the Data Science Virtual Machine image in the Azure Marketplace.

2. Click the Get It Now button.

3. Fill in the details of the VM (give it a name, choose SSD disk over HDD, an SSH username/password, the subscription you'll be billing the instance to, and set the location to be the nearest to you that offers the NC instance type).

4. Click the Create option. The instance should be provisioned in about five minutes.

5. You can use SSH with the username/password that you specified to that instance's public Domain Name System (DNS) name.

6. Jupyter Notebook should run when the instance is provisioned; navigate to *http://dns name of instance:8000* and use the username/password combination that you used for SSH to log in.

Google Cloud Platform

In addition to offering K80, P100, and V100-backed instances like Amazon and Azure, Google Cloud Platform (GCP) offers the aforementioned TPUs for those who have tremendous data and compute requirements. You don't need TPUs for this book, and they are pricey, but they *will* work with PyTorch 1.0, so don't think that you have to use TensorFlow in order to take advantage of them if you have a project that requires their use.

Getting started with Google Cloud is also pretty easy:

1. Search for Deep Learning VM on the GCP Marketplace.

2. Click Launch on Compute Engine.

3. Give the instance a name and assign it to the region closest to you.

4. Set the machine type to 8 vCPUs.

5. Set GPU to 1 K80.

6. Ensure that PyTorch 1.0 is selected in the Framework section.

7. Select the "Install NVIDIA GPU automatically on first startup?" checkbox.

8. Set Boot disk to SSD Persistent Disk.

9. Click the Deploy option. The VM will take about 5 minutes to fully deploy.

10. To connect to Jupyter on the instance, make sure you're logged into the correct project in `gcloud` and issue this command:

```
gcloud compute ssh _INSTANCE_NAME_ -- -L 8080:localhost:8080
```

The charges for Google Cloud should work out to about 70 cents an hour, making it the cheapest of the three major cloud providers.

Which Cloud Provider Should I Use?

If you have nothing pulling you in any direction, I recommend Google Cloud Platform (GCP); it's the cheapest option, and you can scale all the way up to using TPUs if required, with a lot more flexibility than either the AWS or Azure offerings. But if you have resources on one of the other two platforms already, you'll be absolutely fine running in those environments.

Once you have your cloud instance running, you'll be able to log in to its copy of Jupyter Notebook, so let's take a look at that next.

Using Jupyter Notebook

If you haven't come across it before, here's the lowdown on Jupyter Notebook: this browser-based environment allows you to mix live code with text, images, and visualizations and has become one of the de facto tools of data scientists all over the world. Notebooks created in Jupyter can be easily shared; indeed, you'll find all the notebooks in this book (*https://oreil.ly/iBh4V*). You can see a screenshot of Jupyter Notebook in action in Figure 1-2.

We won't be using any advanced features of Jupyter in this book; all you need to know is how to create a new notebook and that Shift-Enter runs the contents of a cell. But if you've never used it before, I suggest browsing the Jupyter documentation (*https://oreil.ly/-Yhff*) before you get to Chapter 2.

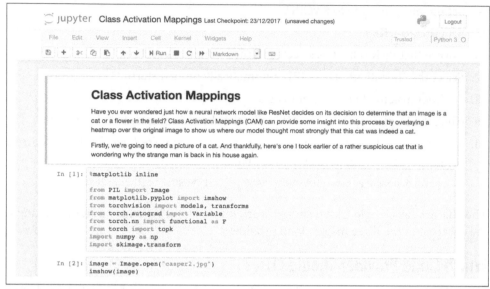

Figure 1-2. Jupyter Notebook

Before we get into using PyTorch, we'll cover one last thing: how to install everything manually.

Installing PyTorch from Scratch

Perhaps you want a little more control over your software than using one of the preceding cloud-provided images. Or you need a particular version of PyTorch for your code. Or, despite all my cautionary warnings, you really want that rig in your basement. Let's look at how to install PyTorch on a Linux server in general.

 You can use PyTorch with Python 2.*x*, but I strongly recommend against doing so. While the Python 2.*x* to 3.*x* upgrade saga has been running for over a decade now, more and more packages are beginning to drop Python 2.*x* support. So unless you have a good reason, make sure your system is running Python 3.

Download CUDA

Although PyTorch can be run entirely in CPU mode, in most cases, GPU-powered PyTorch is required for practical usage, so we're going to need GPU support. This is fairly straightforward; assuming you have an NVIDIA card, this is provided by their Compute Unified Device Architecture (CUDA) API. Download the appropriate package format (*https://oreil.ly/Gx_q2*) for your flavor of Linux and install the package.

For Red Hat Enterprise Linux (RHEL) 7:

```
sudo rpm -i cuda-repo-rhel7-10-0local-10.0.130-410.48-1.0-1.x86_64.rpm
sudo yum clean all
sudo yum install cuda
```

For Ubuntu 18.04:

```
sudo dpkg -i cuda-repo-ubuntu1804-10-0-local-10.0.130-410.48_1.0-1_amd64.deb
sudo apt-key add /var/cuda-repo-<version>/7fa2af80.pub
sudo apt-get update
sudo apt-get install cuda
```

Anaconda

Python has a variety of packaging systems, all of which have good and not-so-good points. Like the developers of PyTorch, I recommend that you install Anaconda, a packaging system dedicated to producing the best distribution of packages for data scientists. Like CUDA, it's fairly easy to install.

Head to Anaconda (*https://oreil.ly/9hAxg*) and pick out the installation file for your machine. Because it's a massive archive that executes via a shell script on your system, I encourage you to run `md5sum` on the file you've downloaded and check it against the list of signatures (*https://oreil.ly/anuhu*) before you execute it with `bash Anaconda3-VERSION-Linux-x86_64.sh` to make sure that the signature on your machine matches the one on the web page. This ensures that the downloaded file hasn't been tampered with and means it's safe to run on your system. The script will present several prompts about locations it'll be installing into; unless there's a good reason, just accept the defaults.

> You might be wondering, "Can I do this on my MacBook?" Sadly, most Macs come with either Intel or AMD GPUs these days and don't really have the support for running PyTorch in GPU-accelerated mode. I recommend using Colab or a cloud provider rather than attempting to use your Mac locally.

Finally, PyTorch! (and Jupyter Notebook)

Now that you have Anaconda installed, getting set up with PyTorch is simple:

```
conda install pytorch torchvision -c pytorch
```

This installs PyTorch and the `torchvision` library that we use in the next couple of chapters to create deep learning architectures that work with images. Anaconda has also installed Jupyter Notebook for us, so we can begin by starting it:

```
jupyter notebook
```

Head to *http://YOUR-IP-ADDRESS:8888* in your browser, create a new notebook, and enter the following:

```
import torch
print(torch.cuda.is_available())
print(torch.rand(2,2))
```

This should produce output similar to this:

```
True
 0.6040  0.6647
 0.9286  0.4210
[torch.FloatTensor of size 2x2]
```

If `cuda.is_available()` returns `False`, you need to debug your CUDA installation so PyTorch can see your graphics card. The values of the tensor will be different on your instance.

But what is this tensor? Tensors are at the heart of almost everything in PyTorch, so you need to know what they are and what they can do for you.

Tensors

A *tensor* is both a container for numbers as well as a set of rules that define transformations between tensors that produce new tensors. It's probably easiest for us to think about *tensors* as multidimensional arrays. Every tensor has a *rank* that corresponds to its dimensional space. A simple scalar (e.g., 1) can be represented as a tensor of rank 0, a vector is rank 1, an $n \times n$ matrix is rank 2, and so on. In the previous example, we created a rank 2 tensor with random values by using `torch.rand()`. We can also create them from lists:

```
x = torch.tensor([[0,0,1],[1,1,1],[0,0,0]])
x
>tensor([[0, 0, 1],
    [1, 1, 1],
    [0, 0, 0]])
```

We can change an element in a tensor by using standard Python indexing:

```
x[0][0] = 5
>tensor([[5, 0, 1],
    [1, 1, 1],
    [0, 0, 0]])
```

You can use special creation functions to generate particular types of tensors. In particular, `ones()` and `zeroes()` will generate tensors filled with 1s and 0s, respectively:

```
torch.zeros(2,2)
> tensor([[0., 0.],
    [0., 0.]])
```

You can perform standard mathematical operations with tensors (e.g., adding two tensors together):

```
tensor.ones(1,2) + tensor.ones(1,2)
> tensor([[2., 2.]])
```

And if you have a tensor of rank 0, you can pull out the value with item():

```
torch.rand(1).item()
> 0.34106671810150146
```

Tensors can live in the CPU or on the GPU and can be copied between devices by using the to() function:

```
cpu_tensor = tensor.rand(2)
cpu_tensor.device
> device(type='cpu')

gpu_tensor = cpu_tensor.to("cuda")
gpu_tensor.device
> device(type='cuda', index=0)
```

Tensor Operations

If you look at the PyTorch documentation (*https://oreil.ly/1Ev0-*), you'll see that there are a *lot* of functions that you can apply to tensors—everything from finding the maximum element to applying a Fourier transform. In this book, you don't need to know all of those in order to turn images, text, and audio into tensors and manipulate them to perform our operations, but you will need some. I definitely recommend that you give the documentation a glance, especially after finishing this book. Now we're going to go through all the functions that will be used in upcoming chapters.

First, we often need to find the maximum item in a tensor as well as the *index* that contains the maximum value (as this often corresponds to the class that the neural network has decided upon in its final prediction). These can be done with the max() and argmax() functions. We can also use item() to extract a standard Python value from a 1D tensor.

```
torch.rand(2,2).max()
> tensor(0.4726)
torch.rand(2,2).max().item()
> 0.8649941086769104
```

Sometimes, we'd like to change the type of a tensor; for example, from a LongTensor to a FloatTensor. We can do this with to():

```
long_tensor = torch.tensor([[0,0,1],[1,1,1],[0,0,0]])
long_tensor.type()
> 'torch.LongTensor'
float_tensor = torch.tensor([[0,0,1],[1,1,1],[0,0,0]]).to(dtype=torch.float32)
```

```
float_tensor.type()
> 'torch.FloatTensor'
```

Most functions that operate on a tensor and return a tensor create a new tensor to store the result. However, if you want to save memory, look to see if an *in-place* function is defined, which should be the same name as the original function but with an appended underscore (_).

```
random_tensor = torch.rand(2,2)
random_tensor.log2()
>tensor([[-1.9001, -1.5013],
        [-1.8836, -0.5320]])
random_tensor.log2_()
> tensor([[-1.9001, -1.5013],
        [-1.8836, -0.5320]])
```

Another common operation is *reshaping* a tensor. This can often occur because your neural network layer may require a slightly different input shape than what you currently have to feed into it. For example, the Modified National Institute of Standards and Technology (MNIST) dataset of handwritten digits is a collection of 28 × 28 images, but the way it's packaged is in arrays of length 784. To use the networks we are constructing, we need to turn those back into 1 × 28 × 28 tensors (the leading 1 is the number of channels—normally red, green, and blue—but as MNIST digits are just grayscale, we have only one channel). We can do this with either view() or reshape():

```
flat_tensor = torch.rand(784)
viewed_tensor = flat_tensor.view(1,28,28)
viewed_tensor.shape
> torch.Size([1, 28, 28])
reshaped_tensor = flat_tensor.reshape(1,28,28)
reshaped_tensor.shape
> torch.Size([1, 28, 28])
```

Note that the reshaped tensor's shape has to have the same number of total elements as the original. If you try flat_tensor.reshape(3,28,28), you'll see an error like this:

```
RuntimeError Traceback (most recent call last)
<ipython-input-26-774c70ba5c08> in <module>()
----> 1 flat_tensor.reshape(3,28,28)

RuntimeError: shape '[3, 28, 28]' is invalid for input of size 784
```

Now you might wonder what the difference is between view() and reshape(). The answer is that view() operates as a view on the original tensor, so if the underlying data is changed, the view will change too (and vice versa). However, view() can throw errors if the required view is not *contiguous*; that is, it doesn't share the same block of memory it would occupy if a new tensor of the required shape was created from scratch. If this happens, you have to call tensor.contiguous() before you can

---

use `view()`. However, `reshape()` does all that behind the scenes, so in general, I recommend using `reshape()` rather than `view()`.

Finally, you might need to rearrange the dimensions of a tensor. You will likely come across this with images, which often are stored as `[height, width, channel]` tensors, but PyTorch prefers to deal with these in a `[channel, height, width]`. You can user `permute()` to deal with these in a fairly straightforward manner:

```
hwc_tensor = torch.rand(640, 480, 3)
chw_tensor = hwc_tensor.permute(2,0,1)
chw_tensor.shape
> torch.Size([3, 640, 480])
```

Here, we've just applied `permute` to a `[640,480,3]` tensor, with the arguments being the indexes of the tensor's dimensions, so we want the final dimension (2, due to zero indexing) to be at the front of our tensor, followed by the remaining two dimensions in their original order.

Tensor Broadcasting

Borrowed from NumPy, *broadcasting* allows you to perform operations between a tensor and a smaller tensor. You can broadcast across two tensors if, starting backward from their trailing dimensions:

- The two dimensions are equal.
- One of the dimensions is 1.

In our use of broadcasting, it works because 1 has a dimension of 1, and as there are no other dimensions, the 1 can be expanded to cover the other tensor. If we tried to add a `[2,2]` tensor to a `[3,3]` tensor, we'd get this error message:

```
The size of tensor a (2) must match the size of
tensor b (3) at non-singleton dimension 1
```

But we could add a `[1,3]` tensor to the `[3,3]` tensor without any trouble. Broadcasting is a handy little feature that increases brevity of code, and is often faster than manually expanding the tensor yourself.

That wraps up everything concerning tensors that you need to get started! We'll cover a few other operations as we come across them later in the book, but this is enough for you to dive into Chapter 2.

Conclusion

Whether it's in the cloud or on your local machine, you should now have PyTorch installed. I've introduced the fundamental building block of the library, *the tensor*, and you've had a brief look at Jupyter Notebook. This is all you need to get started! In the next chapter, you use everything you've seen so far to start building neural networks and classifying images, so make you sure you're comfortable with tensors and Jupyter before moving on.

Further Reading

- Project Jupyter documentation (*https://jupyter.org/documentation*)
- PyTorch documentation (*https://pytorch.org/docs/stable*)
- AWS Deep Learning AMIs (*https://oreil.ly/G9Ldx*)
- Azure Data Science Virtual Machines (*https://oreil.ly/YjzVB*)
- Google Deep Learning VM Image (*https://oreil.ly/NFpeG*)

CHAPTER 2
Image Classification with PyTorch

After you've set up PyTorch, deep learning textbooks normally throw a bunch of jargon at you before doing anything interesting. I try to keep that to a minimum and work through an example, albeit one that can easily be expanded as you get more comfortable working with PyTorch. We use this example throughout the book to demonstrate how to debug a model (Chapter 7) or deploy it to production (Chapter 8).

What we're going to construct from now until the end of Chapter 4 is an *image classifier*. Neural networks are commonly used as image classifiers; the network is given a picture and asked what is, to us, a simple question: "What is this?"

Let's get started with building our PyTorch application.

Our Classification Problem

Here we build a simple classifier that can tell the difference between fish and cats. We'll be iterating over the design and how we build our model to make it more and more accurate.

Figures 2-1 and 2-2 show a fish and a cat in all their glory. I'm not sure whether the fish has a name, but the cat is called Helvetica.

Let's begin with a discussion of the traditional challenges involved in classification.

Figure 2-1. A fish!

Figure 2-2. Helvetica in a box

Traditional Challenges

How would you go about writing a program that could tell a fish from a cat? Maybe you'd write a set of rules describing that a cat has a tail, or that a fish has scales, and apply those rules to an image to determine what you're looking at. But that would take time, effort, and skill. Plus, what happens if you encounter something like a Manx cat; while it is clearly a cat, it doesn't have a tail.

You can see how these rules are just going get more and more complicated to describe all possible scenarios. Also, I'll admit that I'm absolutely terrible at graphics programming, so the idea of having to manually code all these rules fills me with dread.

What we're after is a function that, given the input of an image, returns *cat* or *fish*. That function is hard for us to construct by exhaustively listing all the criteria. But deep learning essentially makes the computer do all the hard work of constructing all those rules that we just talked about—provided we create a structure, give the network lots of data, and give it a way to work out whether it is getting the right answer. So that's what we're going to do. Along the way, you'll learn some key concepts of how to use PyTorch.

But First, Data

First, we need data. How much data? Well, that depends. The idea that for any deep learning technique to work, you need vast quantities of data to train the neural network is not necessarily true, as you'll see in Chapter 4. However, right now we're going to be training from scratch, which often does require access to a large quantity of data. We need a lot of pictures of fish and cats.

Now, we could spend some time downloading many images from something like Google image search, but in this instance we have a shortcut: a standard collection of images used to train neural networks, called *ImageNet*. It contains more than 14 million images and 20,000 image categories. It's the standard that all image classifiers judge themselves against. So I take images from there, though feel free to download other ones yourself if you prefer.

Along with the data, PyTorch needs a way to determine what is a cat and what is a fish. That's easy enough for us, but it's somewhat harder for the computer (which is why we are building the program in the first place!). We use a *label* attached to the data, and training in this manner is called *supervised learning*. (When you don't have access to any labels, you have to use, perhaps unsurprisingly, *unsupervised learning* methods for training.)

Now, if we're using ImageNet data, its labels aren't going to be all that useful, because they contain *too* much information for us. A label of *tabby cat* or *trout* is, to the computer, separate from *cat* or *fish*. We'll need to relabel these. Because ImageNet is such a vast collection of images, I have pulled together a list of image URLs and labels (*https://oreil.ly/NbtEU*) for both fish and cats.

You can run the *download.py* script in that directory, and it will download the images from the URLs and place them in the appropriate locations for training. The *relabeling* is simple; the script stores cat pictures in the directory *train/cat* and fish pictures in *train/fish*. If you'd prefer to not use the script for downloading, just create these directories and put the appropriate pictures in the right locations. We now have our data, but we need to get it into a format that PyTorch can understand.

PyTorch and Data Loaders

Loading and converting data into formats that are ready for training can often end up being one of the areas in data science that sucks up far too much of our time. PyTorch has developed standard conventions of interacting with data that make it fairly consistent to work with, whether you're working with images, text, or audio.

The two main conventions of interacting with data are *datasets* and *data loaders*. A *dataset* is a Python class that allows us to get at the data we're supplying to the neural network. A *data loader* is what feeds data from the dataset into the network. (This can encompass information such as, *How many worker processes are feeding data into the network?* or *How many images are we passing in at once?*)

Let's look at the dataset first. Every dataset, no matter whether it includes images, audio, text, 3D landscapes, stock market information, or whatever, can interact with PyTorch if it satisfies this abstract Python class:

```
class Dataset(object):
    def __getitem__(self, index):
        raise NotImplementedError

    def __len__(self):
        raise NotImplementedError
```

This is fairly straightforward: we have to implement a method that returns the size of our dataset (`len`), and implement a method that can retrieve an item from our dataset in a (`label`, `tensor`) pair. This is called by the data loader as it is pushing data into the neural network for training. So we have to write a body for `getitem` that can take an image and transform it into a tensor and return that and the label back so PyTorch can operate on it. This is fine, but you can imagine that this scenario comes up a lot, so maybe PyTorch can make things easier for us?

Building a Training Dataset

The `torchvision` package includes a class called `ImageFolder` that does pretty much everything for us, providing our images are in a structure where each directory is a label (e.g., all cats are in a directory called *cat*). For our cats and fish example, here's what you need:

```
import torchvision
from torchvision import transforms

train_data_path = "./train/"

transforms = transforms.Compose([
    transforms.Resize(64),
    transforms.ToTensor(),
    transforms.Normalize(mean=[0.485, 0.456, 0.406],
              std=[0.229, 0.224, 0.225] )
    ])

train_data = torchvision.datasets.ImageFolder
(root=train_data_path,transform=transforms)
```

A little bit more is going on here because `torchvision` also allows you to specify a list of transforms that will be applied to an image before it gets fed into the neural network. The default transform is to take image data and turn it into a tensor (the `trans forms.ToTensor()` method seen in the preceding code), but we're also doing a couple of other things that might not seem obvious.

Firstly, GPUs are built to be fast at performing calculations that are a standard size. But we probably have an assortment of images at many resolutions. To increase our processing performance, we scale every incoming image to the same resolution of 64 × 64 via the `Resize(64)` transform. We then convert the images to a tensor, and finally, we normalize the tensor around a specific set of mean and standard deviation points.

Normalizing is important because a lot of multiplication will be happening as the input passes through the layers of the neural network; keeping the incoming values between 0 and 1 prevents the values from getting too large during the training phase (known as the *exploding gradient* problem). And that magic incarnation is just the mean and standard deviation of the ImageNet dataset as a whole. You could calculate it specifically for this fish and cat subset, but these values are decent enough. (If you were working on a completely different dataset, you'd have to calculate that mean and deviation, although many people just use these ImageNet constants and report acceptable results.)

The composable transforms also allow us to easily do things like image rotation and skewing for data augmentation, which we'll come back to in Chapter 4.

We're resizing the images to 64 × 64 in this example. I've made that arbitrary choice in order to make the computation in our upcoming first network fast. Most existing architectures that you'll see in Chapter 3 use 224 × 224 or 299 × 299 for their image inputs. In general, the larger the input size, the more data for the network to learn from. The flip side is that you can often fit a smaller batch of images within the GPU's memory.

We're not quite done with datasets yet. But why do we need more than just a training dataset?

Building Validation and Test Datasets

Our training data is set up, but we need to repeat the same steps for our *validation* data. What's the difference here? One danger of deep learning (and all machine learning, in fact) is the concept of *overfitting*: your model gets really good at recognizing what it has been trained on, but cannot generalize to examples it hasn't seen. So it sees a picture of a cat, and unless all other pictures of cats resemble that picture very closely, the model doesn't think it's a cat, despite it obviously being so. To prevent our network from doing this, we download a *validation set* in *download.py*, which is a series of cat and fish pictures that do not occur in the training set. At the end of each training cycle (also known as an *epoch*), we compare against this set to make sure our network isn't getting things wrong. But don't worry—the code for this is incredibly easy because it's just the earlier code with a few variable names changed:

```
val_data_path = "./val/"
val_data = torchvision.datasets.ImageFolder(root=val_data_path,
                                            transform=transforms)
```

We just reused the `transforms` chain instead of having to define it once again.

In addition to a validation set, we should also create a *test set*. This is used to test the model after all training has been completed:

```
test_data_path = "./test/"
test_data = torchvision.datasets.ImageFolder(root=test_data_path,
                                             transform=transforms)
```

Distinguishing the types of sets can be a little confusing, so I've compiled a table to indicate which set is used for which part of model training; see Table 2-1.

Table 2-1. Dataset types

Training set	Used in the training pass to update the model
Validation set	Used to evaluate how the model is generalizing to the problem domain, rather than fitting to the training data; not used to update the model directly
Test set	A final dataset that provides a final evaluation of the model's performance after training is complete

We can then build our data loaders with a few more lines of Python:

```
batch_size=64
train_data_loader = data.DataLoader(train_data, batch_size=batch_size)
val_data_loader  = data.DataLoader(val_data, batch_size=batch_size)
test_data_loader  = data.DataLoader(test_data, batch_size=batch_size)
```

The new thing to note from this code is `batch_size`. This tells us how many images will go through the network before we train and update it. We could, in theory, set the `batch_size` to the number of images in the test and training sets so the network sees every image before it updates. In practice, we tend not to do this because smaller batches (more commonly known as *mini-batches* in the literature) require less memory than having to store all the information about *every* image in the dataset, and the smaller batch size ends up making training faster as we're updating our network much more quickly.

By default, PyTorch's data loaders are set to a `batch_size` of 1. You will almost certainly want to change that. Although I've chosen 64 here, you might want to experiment to see how big of a minibatch you can use without exhausting your GPU's memory. You may also want to experiment with some of the additional parameters: you can specify how datasets are sampled, whether the entire set is shuffled on each run, and how many worker processes are used to pull data out of the dataset. This can all be found in the PyTorch documentation (*https://oreil.ly/XORs1*).

That covers getting data into PyTorch, so let's now introduce a simple neural network to actually start classifying our images.

Finally, a Neural Network!

We're going to start with the simplest deep learning network: an input layer, which will work on the input tensors (our images); our output layer, which will be the size of the number of our output classes (2); and a hidden layer between them. In our first example, we'll use fully connected layers. Figure 2-3 illustrates what that looks like with an input layer of three nodes, a hidden layer of three nodes, and our two-node output.

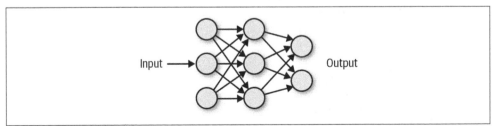

Figure 2-3. A simple neural network

As you can see, in this fully connected example, every node in a layer affects every node in the next layer, and each connection has a *weight* that determines the strength of the signal from that node going into the next layer. (It is these weights that will be updated when we train the network, normally from a random initialization.) As an input passes through the network, we (or PyTorch) can simply do a matrix multiplication of the weights and biases of that layer onto the input. Before feeding it into the next function, that result goes into an *activation function*, which is simply a way of inserting nonlinearity into our system.

Activation Functions

Activation functions sound complicated, but the most common activation function you'll come across in the literature these days is ReLU, or *rectified linear unit*. Which again sounds complicated! But all it turns out to be is a function that implements *max(0,x)*, so the result is 0 if the input is negative, or just the input (*x*) if *x* is positive. Simple!

Another activation function you'll likely come across is *softmax*, which is a little more complicated mathematically. Basically it produces a set of values between 0 and 1 that adds up to 1 (probabilities!) and weights the values so it exaggerates differences—that is, it produces one result in a vector higher than everything else. You'll often see it being used at the end of a classification network to ensure that that network makes a definite prediction about what class it thinks the input belongs to.

With all these building blocks in place, we can start to build our first neural network.

Creating a Network

Creating a network in PyTorch is a very Pythonic affair. We inherit from a class called torch.nn.Network and fill out the __init__ and forward methods:

```
class SimpleNet(nn.Module):

def __init__(self):
    super(Net, self).__init__()
    self.fc1 = nn.Linear(12288, 84)
    self.fc2 = nn.Linear(84, 50)
    self.fc3 = nn.Linear(50,2)

def forward(self):
    x = x.view(-1, 12288)
    x = F.relu(self.fc1(x))
    x = F.relu(self.fc2(x))
    x = F.softmax(self.fc3(x))
    return x

simplenet = SimpleNet()
```

Again, this is not too complicated. We do any setup required in init(), in this case calling our superclass constructor and the three fully connected layers (called Linear in PyTorch, as opposed to Dense in Keras). The forward() method describes how data flows through the network in both training and making predictions (*inference*). First, we have to convert the 3D tensor (*x* and *y* plus three-channel color information —red, green, blue) in an image, remember!—into a 1D tensor so that it can be fed into the first Linear layer, and we do that using the view(). From there, you can see that we apply the layers and the activation functions in order, finally returning the softmax output to give us our prediction for that image.

The numbers in the hidden layers are somewhat arbitrary, with the exception of the output of the final layer, which is 2, matching up with our two classes of cat or fish. In general, you want the data in your layers to be *compressed* as it goes down the stack. If a layer is going to, say, 50 inputs to 100 outputs, then the network might *learn* by simply passing the 50 connections to 50 of the 100 outputs and consider its job done. By reducing the size of the output with respect to the input, we force that part of the network to learn a representation of the original input with fewer resources, which hopefully means that it extracts some features of the images that are important to the problem we're trying to solve; for example, learning to spot a fin or a tail.

We have a prediction, and we can compare that with the actual label of the original image to see whether the prediction was correct. But we need some way of allowing PyTorch to quantify not just whether a prediction is right or wrong, but just how wrong or right it is. This is handled by a loss function.

Loss Functions

Loss functions are one of the key pieces of an effective deep learning solution. PyTorch uses loss functions to determine how it will update the network to reach the desired results.

Loss functions can be as complicated or as simple as you desire. PyTorch comes complete with a comprehensive collection of them that will cover most of the applications you're likely to encounter, plus of course you can write your own if you have a very custom domain. In our case, we're going to use a built-in loss function called CrossEntropyLoss, which is recommended for multiclass categorization tasks like we're doing here. Another loss function you're likely to come across is MSELoss, which is a standard mean squared loss that you might use when making a numerical prediction.

One thing to be aware of with CrossEntropyLoss is that it also incorporates softmax() as part of its operation, so our forward() method becomes the following:

```
def forward(self):
    # Convert to 1D vector
    x = x.view(-1, 12288)
    x = F.relu(self.fc1(x))
```

```
x = F.relu(self.fc2(x))
x = self.fc3(x)
return x
```

Now let's look at how a neural network's layers are updated during the training loop.

Optimizing

Training a network involves passing data through the network, using the loss function to determine the difference between the prediction and the actual label, and then using that information to update the weights of the network in an attempt to make the loss function return as small a loss as possible. To perform the updates on the neural network, we use an *optimizer*.

If we just had one weight, we could plot a graph of the loss value against the value of the weight, and it might look something like Figure 2-4.

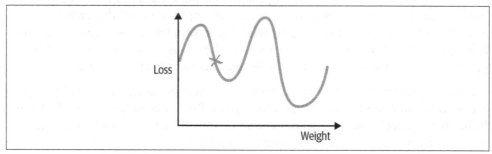

Figure 2-4. A 2D plot of loss

If we start at a random position, marked in Figure 2-4 by the X, with our weight value on the x-axis and the loss function on the y-axis, we need to get to the lowest point on the curve to find our optimal solution. We can move by altering the value of the weight, which will give us a new value for the loss function. To know how good a move we're making, we can check against the gradient of the curve. One common way to visualize the optimizer is like rolling a marble, trying to find the lowest point (or *minima*) in a series of valleys. This is perhaps clearer if we extend our view to two parameters, creating a 3D graph as shown in Figure 2-5.

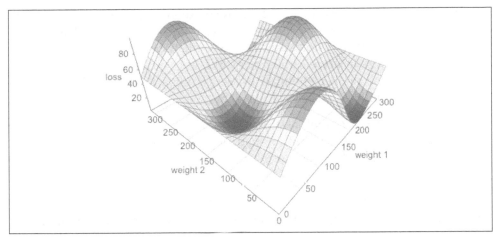

Figure 2-5. A 3D plot of loss

And in this case, at every point, we can check the gradients of all the potential moves and choose the one that moves us most down the hill.

You need to be aware of a couple of issues, though. The first is the danger of getting trapped in *local minima*, areas that look like they're the shallowest parts of the loss curve if we check our gradients, but actually shallower areas exist elsewhere. If we go back to our 1D curve in Figure 2-4, we can see that if we end up in the minima on the left by taking short hops down, we'd never have any reason to leave that position. And if we took giant hops, we might find ourselves getting onto the path that leads to the actual lowest point, but because we keep making jumps that are so big, we keep bouncing all over the place.

The size of our hops is known as the *learning rate*, and is often the *key* parameter that needs to be tweaked in order to get your network learning properly and efficiently. You'll see a way of determining a good learning rate in Chapter 4, but for now, you'll be experimenting with different values: try something like 0.001 to begin with. As just mentioned, large learning rates will cause your network to bounce all over the place in training, and it will not *converge* on a good set of weights.

As for the local minima problem, we make a slight alteration to our taking all the possible gradients and indicate sample random gradients during a batch. Known as *stochastic gradient descent* (SGD), this is the traditional approach to optimizing neural networks and other machine learning techniques. But other optimizers are available, and indeed for deep learning, preferable. PyTorch ships with SGD and others such as AdaGrad and RMSProp, as well as Adam, the optimizer we will be using for the majority of the book.

One of the key improvements that Adam makes (as does RMSProp and AdaGrad) is that it uses a learning rate per parameter, and adapts that learning rate depending on the rate of change of those parameters. It keeps an exponentially decaying list of gradients and the square of those gradients and uses those to scale the global learning rate that Adam is working with. Adam has been empirically shown to outperform most other optimizers in deep learning networks, but you can swap out Adam for SGD or RMSProp or another optimizer to see if using a different technique yields faster and better training for your particular application.

Creating an Adam-based optimizer is simple. We call `optim.Adam()` and pass in the weights of the network that it will be updating (obtained via `simplenet.parame ters()`) and our example learning rate of 0.001:

```
import torch.optim as optim
optimizer = optim.Adam(simplenet.parameters(), lr=0.001)
```

The optimizer is the last piece of the puzzle, so we can finally start training our network.

Training

Here's our complete training loop, which combines everything you've seen so far to train the network. We're going to write this as a function so parts such as the loss function and optimizer can be passed in as parameters. It looks quite generic at this point:

```
for epoch in range(epochs):
    for batch in train_loader:
        optimizer.zero_grad()
        input, target = batch
        output = model(input)
        loss = loss_fn(output, target)
        loss.backward()
        optimizer.step()
```

It's fairly straightforward, but you should note a few things. We take a batch from our training set on every iteration of the loop, which is handled by our data loader. We then run those through our model and compute the loss from the expected output. To compute the gradients, we call the `backward()` method on the model. The `opti mizer.step()` method uses those gradients afterward to perform the adjustment of the weights that we talked about in the previous section.

What is that `zero_grad()` call doing, though? It turns out that the calculated gradients accumulate by default, meaning that if we didn't zero the gradients at the end of the batch's iteration, the next batch would have to deal with this batch's gradients as well as its own, and the batch after that would have to cope with the previous two, and so on. This isn't helpful, as we want to look at only the gradients of the current batch for our optimization in each iteration. We use `zero_grad()` to make sure they are reset to zero after we're done with our loop.

That's the abstracted version of the training loop, but we have to address a few more things before we can write our complete function.

Making It Work on the GPU

If you've run any of the code so far, you might have noticed that it's not all that fast. What about that shiny GPU that's sitting attached to our instance in the cloud (or the very expensive machine we've put together on our desktop)? PyTorch, by default, does CPU-based calculations. To take advantage of the GPU, we need to move our input tensors and the model itself to the GPU by explicitly using the to() method. Here's an example that copies the SimpleNet to the GPU:

```
if torch.cuda.is_available():
        device = torch.device("cuda")
else
    device = torch.device("cpu")

model.to(device)
```

Here, we copy the model to the GPU if PyTorch reports that one is available, or otherwise keep the model on the CPU. By using this construction, we can determine whether a GPU is available at the start of our code and use tensor| model.to(device) throughout the rest of the program, being confident that it will go to the correct place.

In earlier versions of PyTorch, you would use the cuda() method to copy data to the GPU instead. If you come across that method when looking at other people's code, just be aware that it's doing the same thing as to()!

And that wraps up all the steps required for training. We're almost done!

Putting It All Together

You've seen a lot of different pieces of code throughout this chapter, so let's consolidate it. We put it all together to create a generic training method that takes in a model, as well as training and validation data, along with learning rate and batch size options, and performs training on that model. We use this code throughout the rest of the book:

```
def train(model, optimizer, loss_fn, train_loader, val_loader,
epochs=20, device="cpu"):
    for epoch in range(epochs):
        training_loss = 0.0
        valid_loss = 0.0
        model.train()
```

```
for batch in train_loader:
    optimizer.zero_grad()
    inputs, target = batch
    inputs = inputs.to(device)
    target = targets.to(device)
    output = model(inputs)
    loss = loss_fn(output, target)
    loss.backward()
    optimizer.step()
    training_loss += loss.data.item()
training_loss /= len(train_iterator)

model.eval()
num_correct = 0
num_examples = 0
for batch in val_loader:
    inputs, targets = batch
    inputs = inputs.to(device)
    output = model(inputs)
    targets = targets.to(device)
    loss = loss_fn(output,targets)
    valid_loss += loss.data.item()
    correct = torch.eq(torch.max(F.softmax(output), dim=1)[1],
                                        target).view(-1)
    num_correct += torch.sum(correct).item()
    num_examples += correct.shape[0]
valid_loss /= len(valid_iterator)

print('Epoch: {}, Training Loss: {:.2f},
Validation Loss: {:.2f},
accuracy = {:.2f}'.format(epoch, training_loss,
valid_loss, num_correct / num_examples))
```

That's our training function, and we can kick off training by calling it with the required parameters:

```
train(simplenet, optimizer, torch.nn.CrossEntropyLoss(),
    train_data_loader, test_data_loader,device)
```

The network will train for 20 epochs (you can adjust this by passing in a value for epoch to `train()`), and you should get a printout of the model's accuracy on the validation set at the end of each epoch.

You have trained your first neural network—congratulations! You can now use it to make predictions, so let's look at how to do that.

Making Predictions

Way back at the start of the chapter, I said we would make a neural network that could classify whether an image is a cat or a fish. We've now trained one to do just that, but how do we use it to generate a prediction for a single image? Here's a quick bit of Python code that will load an image from the filesystem and print out whether our network says *cat* or *fish*:

```
from PIL import Image

labels = ['cat','fish']

img = Image.open(FILENAME)
img = transforms(img)
img = img.unsqueeze(0)

prediction = simplenet(img)
prediction = prediction.argmax()
print(labels[prediction])
```

Most of this code is straightforward; we reuse the transform pipeline we made earlier to convert the image into the correct form for our neural network. However, because our network uses batches, it actually expects a 4D tensor, with the first dimension denoting the different images within a batch. We don't have a batch, but we can create a batch of length 1 by using unsqueeze(0), which adds a new dimension at the front of our tensor.

Getting predictions is as simple as passing our *batch* into the model. We then have to find out the class with the higher probability. In this case, we could simply convert the tensor to an array and compare the two elements, but there are often many more than that. Helpfully, PyTorch provides the argmax() function, which returns the index of the highest value of the tensor. We then use that to index into our labels array and print out our prediction. As an exercise, use the preceding code as a basis to work out predictions on the test set that we created at the start of the chapter. You don't need to use unsqueeze() because you get batches from the test_data_loader.

That's about all you need to know about making predictions for now; we return to this in Chapter 8 when we harden things for production usage.

In addition to making predictions, we probably would like to be able to reload the model at any point in the future with our trained parameters, so let's take a look at how that's done with PyTorch.

Model Saving

If you're happy with the performance of a model or need to stop for any reason, you can save the current state of a model in Python's *pickle* format by using the torch.save() method. Conversely, you can load a previously saved iteration of a model by using the torch.load() method.

Saving our current parameters and model structure would therefore work like this:

```
torch.save(simplenet, "/tmp/simplenet")
```

And we can reload as follows:

```
simplenet = torch.load("/tmp/simplenet")
```

This stores both the parameters and the structure of the model to a file. This might be a problem if you change the structure of the model at a later point. For this reason, it's more common to save a model's `state_dict` instead. This is a standard Python `dict` that contains the maps of each layer's parameters in the model. Saving the `state_dict` looks like this:

```
torch.save(model.state_dict(), PATH)
```

To restore, create an instance of the model first and then use `load_state_dict`. For `SimpleNet`:

```
simplenet = SimpleNet()
simplenet_state_dict = torch.load("/tmp/simplenet")
simplenet.load_state_dict(simplenet_state_dict)
```

The benefit here is that if you extend the model in some fashion, you can supply a `strict=False` parameter to `load_state_dict` that assigns parameters to layers in the model that do exist in the `state_dict`, but does not fail if the loaded `state_dict` has layers missing or added from the model's current structure. Because it's just a normal Python `dict`, you can change the key names to fit your model, which can be handy if you are pulling in parameters from a completely different model altogether.

Models can be saved to a disk during a training run and reloaded at another point so that training can continue where you left off. That is quite useful when using something like Google Colab, which lets you have continuous access to a GPU for only around 12 hours. By keeping track of time, you can save the model before the cutoff and continue training in a new 12-hour session.

Conclusion

You've taken a whirlwind tour through the basics of neural networks and learned how, using PyTorch, you can train them with a dataset, make predictions on other images, and save/restore models to and from disk.

Before you read the next chapter, experiment with the `SimpleNet` architecture we created here. Adjust the number of parameters in the `Linear` layers, and maybe add another layer or two. Have a look at the various activation functions available in PyTorch and swap out `ReLU` for something else. See what happens to training if you adjust the learning rate or switch out the optimizer from Adam to another option (perhaps try vanilla SGD). Maybe alter the batch size and the initial size of the image as it gets turned into a 1D tensor at the start of the forward pass. A lot of deep learning work is still in the phase of artisanal construction; learning rates are tinkered with by hand until a network is trained appropriately, so it's good to get a handle on how all the moving parts interact.

You might be a little disappointed with the accuracy of the `SimpleNet` architecture, but don't worry! Chapter 3 provides some definite improvements as we introduce the convolutional neural network in place of the very simple network we've been using so far.

Further Reading

- PyTorch documentation (*https://oreil.ly/x6pO7*)
- "Adam: A Method for Stochastic Optimization" (*https://arxiv.org/abs/1412.6980*) by Diederik P. Kingma and Jimmy Ba (2014)
- "An Overview of Gradient Descent Optimization Algorithms" (*https://arxiv.org/abs/1609.04747*) by Sebstian Ruder (2016)

CHAPTER 3

Convolutional Neural Networks

After experimenting with the fully connected neural networks in Chapter 2, you probably noticed a few things. If you attempted to add more layers or vastly increase the number of parameters, you almost certainly ran out of memory on your GPU. In addition, it took a while to train to anything resembling somewhat decent accuracy, and even that wasn't much to shout about, especially considering the hype surrounding deep learning. What's going on?

It's true that a fully connected or (*feed-forward*) network can function as a universal approximator, but the theory doesn't say how long it'll take you to train it to become that approximation to the function you're really after. But we can do better, especially with images. In this chapter, you'll learn about *convolutional neural networks* (CNNs) and how they form the backbone of the most accurate image classifiers around today (we take a look at a couple of them in some detail along the way). We build up a new convolutional-based architecture for our fish versus cat application and show that it is quicker to train *and* more accurate than what we were doing in the previous chapter. Let's get started!

Our First Convolutional Model

This time around, I'm going to share the final model architecture first, and then discuss all the new pieces. And as I mentioned in Chapter 2, the training method we created is independent of the model, so you can go ahead and test this model out first and then come back for the explanation!

```
class CNNNet(nn.Module):

    def __init__(self, num_classes=2):
        super(CNNNet, self).__init__()
        self.features = nn.Sequential(
            nn.Conv2d(3, 64, kernel_size=11, stride=4, padding=2),
```

```
        nn.ReLU(),
        nn.MaxPool2d(kernel_size=3, stride=2),
        nn.Conv2d(64, 192, kernel_size=5, padding=2),
        nn.ReLU(),
        nn.MaxPool2d(kernel_size=3, stride=2),
        nn.Conv2d(192, 384, kernel_size=3, padding=1),
        nn.ReLU(),
        nn.Conv2d(384, 256, kernel_size=3, padding=1),
        nn.ReLU(),
        nn.Conv2d(256, 256, kernel_size=3, padding=1),
        nn.ReLU(),
        nn.MaxPool2d(kernel_size=3, stride=2),
    )
    self.avgpool = nn.AdaptiveAvgPool2d((6, 6))
    self.classifier = nn.Sequential(
        nn.Dropout(),
        nn.Linear(256 * 6 * 6, 4096),
        nn.ReLU(),
        nn.Dropout(),
        nn.Linear(4096, 4096),
        nn.ReLU(),
        nn.Linear(4096, num_classes)
    )

def forward(self, x):
    x = self.features(x)
    x = self.avgpool(x)
    x = torch.flatten(x, 1)
    x = self.classifier(x)
    return x
```

The first thing to notice is the use of nn.Sequential(). This allows us to create a chain of layers. When we use one of these chains in forward(), the input goes through each element of the array of layers in succession. You can use this to break your model into more logical arrangements. In this network, we have two chains: the features block and the classifier. Let's take a look at the new layers we're introducing, starting with Conv2d.

Convolutions

The Conv2d layer is a *2D convolution*. If we have a grayscale image, it consists of an array, x pixels wide and y pixels high, with each entry having a value that indicates whether it's black or white or somewhere in between (we assume an 8-bit image, so each value can vary from 0 to 255). For this example we look at a small, square image that's 4 pixels high and wide:

$$\begin{bmatrix} 10 & 11 & 9 & 3 \\ 2 & 123 & 4 & 0 \\ 45 & 237 & 23 & 99 \\ 20 & 67 & 22 & 255 \end{bmatrix}$$

Next we introduce something called a *filter*, or *convolutional kernel*. This is another matrix, most likely smaller, which we will drag across our image. Here's our 2 × 2 filter:

$$\begin{bmatrix} 1 & 0 \\ 1 & 0 \end{bmatrix}$$

To produce our output, we take the smaller filter and pass it over the original input, like a magnifying glass over a piece of paper. Starting from the top left, our first calculation is as follows:

$$\begin{bmatrix} 10 & 11 \\ 2 & 123 \end{bmatrix} \begin{bmatrix} 1 & 0 \\ 1 & 0 \end{bmatrix}$$

And all we do is multiply each element in the matrix by its corresponding member in the other matrix and sum the result: $(10 \times 1) + (11 \times 0) + (2 \times 1) + (123 \times 0) = 12$. Having done that, we move the filter across and begin again. But how much should we move the filter? In this case, we move the filter across by 2, meaning that our second calculation is.

$$\begin{bmatrix} 9 & 3 \\ 4 & 0 \end{bmatrix} \begin{bmatrix} 1 & 0 \\ 1 & 0 \end{bmatrix}$$

This gives us an output of 13. We now move our filter down and back to the left and repeat the process, giving us this final result (or *feature map*):

$$\begin{bmatrix} 12 & 13 \\ 65 & 45 \end{bmatrix}$$

In Figure 3-1, you can see how this works graphically, with a 3 × 3 kernel being dragged across a 4 × 4 tensor and producing a 2 × 2 output (though each segment is based on nine elements instead of the four in our first example).

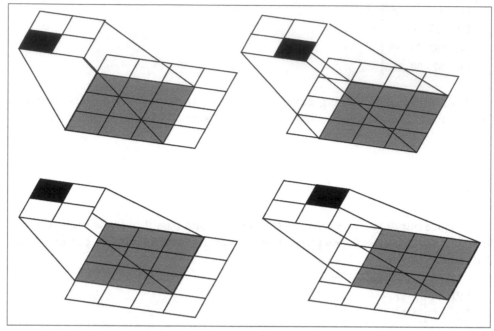

Figure 3-1. How a 3 × 3 kernel operates across a 4 × 4 input

A convolutional layer will have many of these filters, the values of which are filled in by the training of the network, and all the filters in the layer share the same bias values. Let's go back to how we're invoking the Conv2d layer and see some of the other options that we can set:

```
nn.Conv2d(in_channels,out_channels, kernel_size, stride, padding)
```

The in_channels is the number of input channels we'll be receiving in the layer. At the beginning of the network, we're taking in the RGB image as input, so the number of input channels is three. out_channels is, unsurprisingly, the number of output channels, which corresponds to the number of filters in our conv layer. Next is kernel_size, which describes the height and width of our filter.[1] This can be a single scalar specifying a square (e.g., in the first conv layer, we're setting up an 11 × 11 filter), or you can use a tuple (such as (3,5) for a 3 × 5 filter).

The next two parameters seem harmless enough, but they can have big effects on the downstream layers of your network, and even what that particular layer ends up looking at. stride indicates how many steps across the input we move when we adjust the filter to a new position. In our example, we end up with a stride of 2, which has the

---

[1] Kernel and filter tend to be used interchangeably in the literature. If you have experience in graphics processing, kernel is probably more familiar to you, but I prefer filter.

effect of making a feature map that is half the size of the input. But we could have also moved with a stride of 1, which would give us a feature map output of 4 × 4, the same size of the input. We can also pass in a tuple *(a,b)* that would allow us to move *a* across and *b* down on each step. Now, you might be wondering, what happens when it gets to the end? Let's take a look. If we drag our filter along with a stride of 1, we eventually get to this point:

$$\begin{bmatrix} 3 & ? \\ 0 & ? \end{bmatrix}$$

We don't have enough elements in our input to do a full convolution. So what happens? This is where the `padding` parameter comes in. If we give a `padding` value of 1, our input looks a bit like this:

$$\begin{bmatrix} 0 & 0 & 0 & 0 & 0 & 0 \\ 0 & 10 & 11 & 9 & 3 & 0 \\ 0 & 2 & 123 & 4 & 0 & 0 \\ 0 & 45 & 237 & 23 & 99 & 0 \\ 0 & 20 & 67 & 22 & 255 & 0 \\ 0 & 0 & 0 & 0 & 0 & 0 \end{bmatrix}$$

Now when we get to the edge, our values covered by the filter are as follows:

$$\begin{bmatrix} 3 & 0 \\ 0 & 0 \end{bmatrix}$$

If you don't set padding, any edge cases that PyTorch encounters in the last columns of the input are simply thrown away. It's up to you to set padding appropriately. Just as with `stride` and `kernel_size`, you can also pass in a tuple for `height` × `weight` padding instead of a single number that pads the same in both directions.

That's what the `Conv2d` layers are doing in our model. But what about those `Max Pool2d` layers?

Pooling

In conjunction with the convolution layers, you will often see *pooling* layers. These layers reduce the resolution of the network from the previous input layer, which gives us fewer parameters in lower layers. This compression results in faster computation for a start, and it helps prevent overfitting in the network.

In our model, we're using `MaxPool2d` with a kernel size of 3 and a stride of 2. Let's have a look at how that works with an example. Here's a 5 × 3 input:

$$\begin{bmatrix} 1 & 2 & 1 & 4 & 1 \\ 5 & 6 & 1 & 2 & 5 \\ 5 & 0 & 0 & 9 & 6 \end{bmatrix}$$

Using the kernel size of 3 × 3 and a stride of 2, we get two 3 × 3 tensors from the pooling:

$$\begin{bmatrix} 1 & 2 & 1 \\ 5 & 6 & 1 \\ 5 & 0 & 0 \end{bmatrix}$$

$$\begin{bmatrix} 1 & 4 & 1 \\ 1 & 2 & 5 \\ 0 & 9 & 6 \end{bmatrix}$$

In `MaxPool` we take the maximum value from each of these tensors, giving us an output tensor of [6,9]. Just as in the convolutional layers, there's a `padding` option to `Max Pool` that creates a border of zero values around the tensor in case the stride goes outside the tensor window.

As you can imagine, you can pool with other functions aside from taking the maximum value from a kernel. A popular alternative is to take the average of the tensor values, which allows all of the tensor data to contribute to the pool instead of just one value in the `max` case (and if you think about an image, you can imagine that you might want to consider the nearest neighbors of a pixel). Also, PyTorch provides `Adap tiveMaxPool` and `AdaptiveAvgPool` layers, which work independently of the incoming input tensor's dimensions (we have an `AdaptiveAvgPool` in our model, for example). I recommend using these in model architectures that you construct over the standard `MaxPool` or `AvgPool` layers, because they allow you to create architectures that can work with different input dimensions; this is handy when working with disparate datasets.

We have one more new component to talk about, one that is incredibly simple yet important for training.

Dropout

One recurring issue with neural networks is their tendency to overfit to training data, and a large amount of ongoing work is done in the deep learning world to identify approaches that allow networks to learn and generalize to nontraining data without simply learning how to just respond to the training inputs. The Dropout layer is a devilishly simple way of doing this that has the benefit of being easy to understand and effective: what if we just don't train a random bunch of nodes within the network during a training cycle? Because they won't be updated, they won't have the chance to overfit to the input data, and because it's random, each training cycle will ignore a different selection of the input, which should help generalization even further.

By default, the Dropout layers in our example CNN network are initialized with 0.5, meaning that 50% of the input tensor is randomly zeroed out. If you want to change that to 20%, add the p parameter to the initialization call: Dropout(p=0.2).

 Dropout should take place only during training. If it was happening during inference time, you'd lose a chunk of your network's reasoning power, which is not what we want! Thankfully, PyTorch's implementation of Dropout works out which mode you're running in and passes all the data through the Dropout layer at inference time.

Having looked at our little CNN model and examined the layer types in depth, let's take a look at other models that have been made in the past ten years.

History of CNN Architectures

Although CNN models have been around for decades (LeNet-5 was used for digit recognition on check in the late 1990s, for example), it wasn't until GPUs became widely available that deep CNN networks became practical. Even then, it has been only seven years since deep learning networks started to overwhelm all other existing approaches in image classification. In this section, we take a little journey back through the last few years to talk about some milestones in CNN-based learning and investigate some new techniques along the way.

AlexNet

AlexNet was, in many ways, the architecture that changed everything. It was released in 2012 and destroyed all other entries in that year's ImageNet competition with a top-5 error rate of 15.3% (the second place entry had a top-5 error of 26.2%, just to give you an idea of how much better it was than other state-of-the-art methods). AlexNet was one of the first architectures to introduce the concepts of MaxPool and Dropout, and even popularize the then less-well-known ReLU activation function. It was one of the first architectures to demonstrate that many layers were possible and efficient to train on a GPU. Although it's not state of the art anymore, it remains an important milestone in deep learning history.

What does the AlexNet architecture look like? Aha, well, it's time to let you in on a little secret. The network we've been using in this chapter so far? It's AlexNet. Surprise! That's why we used the standard `MaxPool2d` instead of `AdaptiveMaxPool2d`, to match the original AlexNet definition.

Inception/GoogLeNet

Let's skip ahead to the winner of the 2014 ImageNet competition. The GoogLeNet architecture introduced the *Inception* module that addressed some of the deficiencies of AlexNet. In that network, the kernels of the convolutional layers are fixed at a certain resolution. We might expect that an image will have details that are important at both the macro- and microscale. It may be easier to determine whether an object is a car with a large kernel, but to determine whether it's an SUV or a hatchback may require a smaller kernel. And to determine the model, we might need an even smaller kernel to make out details such as logos and insignias.

The Inception network instead runs a series of convolutions of different sizes all on the same input, and concatenates all of the filters together to pass on to the next layer. Before it does any of those, though, it does a 1 × 1 convolution as a *bottleneck* that compresses the input tensor, meaning that the 3 × 3 and 5 × 5 kernels operate on a fewer number of filters than they would if the 1 × 1 convolution wasn't present. You can see an Inception module illustrated in Figure 3-2.

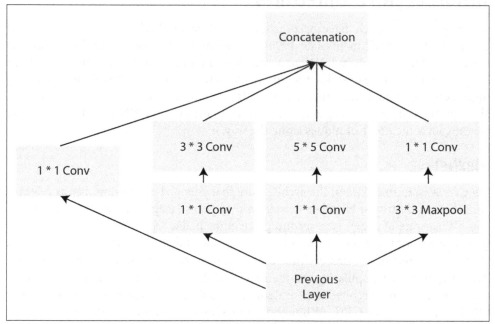

Figure 3-2. An Inception module

The original GoogLeNet architecture uses nine of these modules stacked on top of each other, forming a deep network. Despite the depth, it uses fewer parameters overall than AlexNet while delivering a human-like performance of an 6.67% top-5 error rate.

VGG

The second-place entry in 2014's ImageNet was from the University of Oxford—the Visual Geometry Group (VGG) network. In contrast to GoogLeNet, VGG is a simpler stack of convolutional layers. Coming in various configurations of longer stacks of convolutional filters combined with two large hidden linear layers before the final classification layer, it shows off the power of simple deep architectures (scoring an 8.8% top-5 error in its VGG-16 configuration). Figure 3-3 shows the layers of the VGG-16 from end to end.

The downside of the VGG approach is that the final fully connected layers make the network balloon to a large size, weighing in at 138 million parameters in comparison with GoogLeNet's 7 million. Having said that, the VGG network is still quite popular in the deep learning world despite its huge size, as it's easy to reason about because of its simpler construction and the early availability of trained weights. You'll often see it used in style transfer applications (e.g., turning a photo into a Van Gogh painting) as its combination of convolutional filters do appear to capture that sort of information in a way that's easier to observe than the more complex networks.

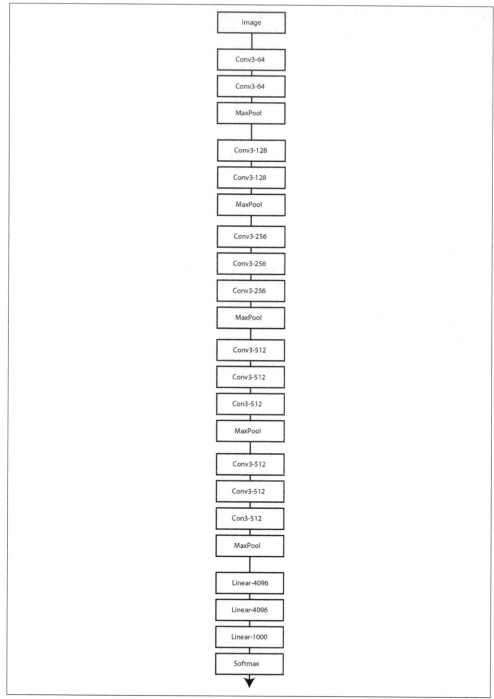

Figure 3-3. VGG-16

ResNet

A year later, Microsoft's ResNet architecture won the ImageNet 2015 competition with a top-5 score of 4.49% in its ResNet-152 variant and 3.57% in an ensemble model (essentially beyond human ability at this point). The innovation that ResNet brought was an improvement on the Inception-style stacking bundle of layers approach, wherein each bundle performed the usual CNN operations but also added the incoming input to the output of the block, as shown in Figure 3-4.

The advantage of this set up is that each block passes through the original input to the next layer, allowing the "signal" of the training data to traverse through deeper networks than possible in either VGG or Inception. (This loss of weight changes in deep networks is known as a *vanishing gradient* because of the gradient changes in back-propagation tending to zero during the training process.)

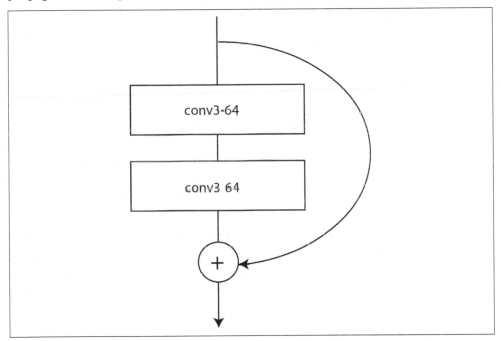

Figure 3-4. A ResNet block

Other Architectures Are Available!

Since 2015 or so, plenty of other architectures have incrementally improved the accuracy on ImageNet, such as DenseNet (an extension of the ResNet idea that allows for the construction of 1,000-layer monster architectures), but also a lot of work has gone into creating architectures such as SqueezeNet and MobileNet, which offer reasonable accuracy but are tiny compared to architectures such as VGG, ResNet, or Inception.

Another big area of research is getting neural networks to start designing neural networks themselves. The most successful attempt so far is, of course, from Google, whose AutoML system generated an architecture called *NASNet* that has a top-5 error rate of 3.8% on ImageNet, which is state of the art as I type this at the start of 2019 (along with another autogenerated architecture from Google called *PNAS*). In fact, the organizers of the ImageNet competition have decided to call a halt to further competitions in this space because the architectures have already gone beyond human levels of ability.

That brings us to the state of the art as of the time this book goes to press, so let's take a look at how we can use these models instead of defining our own.

Using Pretrained Models in PyTorch

Obviously, having to define a model each time you want to use one would be a chore, especially once you move away from AlexNet, so PyTorch provides many of the most popular models by default in the `torchvision` library. For AlexNet, all you need to do is this:

```
import torchvision.models as models
alexnet = models.alexnet(num_classes=2)
```

Definitions for VGG, ResNet, Inception, DenseNet, and SqueezeNet variants are also available. That gives you the model definition, but you can also go a step further and call `models.alexnet(pretrained=True)` to download a pretrained set of weights for AlexNet, allowing you to use it immediately for classification with no extra training. (But as you'll see in the next chapter, you will likely want to do some additional training to improve the accuracy on your particular dataset.)

Having said that, there is something to be said for building the models yourself at least once to get a feel for how they fit together. It's a good way to get some practice building model architectures within PyTorch, and of course you can compare with the provided models to make sure that what you come up with matches the actual definition. But how do you find out what that structure is?

Examining a Model's Structure

If you're curious about how one of these models is constructed, there's an easy way to get PyTorch to help you out. As an example, here's a look at the entire ResNet-18 architecture, which we get by simply calling the following:

```
print(model)

ResNet(
  (conv1): Conv2d(3, 64, kernel_size=(7, 7), stride=(2, 2), padding=(3, 3),
  bias=False)
  (bn1): BatchNorm2d(64, eps=1e-05, momentum=0.1, affine=True,
```

```
  track_running_stats=True)
    (relu): ReLU(inplace)
    (maxpool): MaxPool2d(kernel_size=3, stride=2, padding=1,
    dilation=1, ceil_mode=False)
    (layer1): Sequential(
      (0): BasicBlock(
        (conv1): Conv2d(64, 64, kernel_size=(3, 3), stride=(1, 1),
        padding=(1, 1), bias=False)
        (bn1): BatchNorm2d(64, eps=1e-05, momentum=0.1, affine=True,
        track_running_stats=True)
        (relu): ReLU(inplace)
        (conv2): Conv2d(64, 64, kernel_size=(3, 3), stride=(1, 1),
        padding=(1, 1), bias=False)
        (bn2): BatchNorm2d(64, eps=1e-05, momentum=0.1, affine=True,
        track_running_stats=True)
      )
      (1): BasicBlock(
        (conv1): Conv2d(64, 64, kernel_size=(3, 3), stride=(1, 1),
        padding=(1, 1), bias=False)
        (bn1): BatchNorm2d(64, eps=1e-05, momentum=0.1, affine=True,
        track_running_stats=True)
        (relu): ReLU(inplace)
        (conv2): Conv2d(64, 64, kernel_size=(3, 3), stride=(1, 1),
        padding=(1, 1), bias=False)
        (bn2): BatchNorm2d(64, eps=1e-05, momentum=0.1, affine=True,
        track_running_stats=True)
      )
    )
    (layer2): Sequential(
      (0): BasicBlock(
        (conv1): Conv2d(64, 128, kernel_size=(3, 3), stride=(2, 2),
        padding=(1, 1), bias=False)
        (bn1): BatchNorm2d(128, eps=1e-05, momentum=0.1, affine=True,
        track_running_stats=True)
        (relu): ReLU(inplace)
        (conv2): Conv2d(128, 128, kernel_size=(3, 3), stride=(1, 1),
        padding=(1, 1), bias=False)
        (bn2): BatchNorm2d(128, eps=1e-05, momentum=0.1, affine=True,
        track_running_stats=True)
        (downsample): Sequential(
          (0): Conv2d(64, 128, kernel_size=(1, 1), stride=(2, 2),
          bias=False)
          (1): BatchNorm2d(128, eps=1e-05, momentum=0.1, affine=True,
          track_running_stats=True)
        )
      )
      (1): BasicBlock(
        (conv1): Conv2d(128, 128, kernel_size=(3, 3), stride=(1, 1),
        padding=(1, 1), bias=False)
        (bn1): BatchNorm2d(128, eps=1e-05, momentum=0.1, affine=True,
        track_running_stats=True)
        (relu): ReLU(inplace)
```

```
    (conv2): Conv2d(128, 128, kernel_size=(3, 3), stride=(1, 1),
      padding=(1, 1), bias=False)
    (bn2): BatchNorm2d(128, eps=1e-05, momentum=0.1, affine=True,
    track_running_stats=True)
  )
)
(layer3): Sequential(
  (0): BasicBlock(
    (conv1): Conv2d(128, 256, kernel_size=(3, 3), stride=(2, 2),
      padding=(1, 1), bias=False)
    (bn1): BatchNorm2d(256, eps=1e-05, momentum=0.1, affine=True,
    track_running_stats=True)
    (relu): ReLU(inplace)
    (conv2): Conv2d(256, 256, kernel_size=(3, 3), stride=(1, 1),
    padding=(1, 1), bias=False)
    (bn2): BatchNorm2d(256, eps=1e-05, momentum=0.1, affine=True,
    track_running_stats=True)
    (downsample): Sequential(
      (0): Conv2d(128, 256, kernel_size=(1, 1), stride=(2, 2),
      bias=False)
      (1): BatchNorm2d(256, eps=1e-05, momentum=0.1, affine=True,
      track_running_stats=True)
    )
  )
  (1): BasicBlock(
    (conv1): Conv2d(256, 256, kernel_size=(3, 3), stride=(1, 1),
    padding=(1, 1), bias=False)
    (bn1): BatchNorm2d(256, eps=1e-05, momentum=0.1, affine=True,
    track_running_stats=True)
    (relu): ReLU(inplace)
    (conv2): Conv2d(256, 256, kernel_size=(3, 3), stride=(1, 1),
    padding=(1, 1), bias=False)
    (bn2): BatchNorm2d(256, eps=1e-05, momentum=0.1, affine=True,
    track_running_stats=True)
  )
)
(layer4): Sequential(
  (0): BasicBlock(
    (conv1): Conv2d(256, 512, kernel_size=(3, 3), stride=(2, 2),
    padding=(1, 1), bias=False)
    (bn1): BatchNorm2d(512, eps=1e-05, momentum=0.1, affine=True,
    track_running_stats=True)
    (relu): ReLU(inplace)
    (conv2): Conv2d(512, 512, kernel_size=(3, 3), stride=(1, 1),
    padding=(1, 1), bias=False)
    (bn2): BatchNorm2d(512, eps=1e-05, momentum=0.1, affine=True,
    track_running_stats=True)
    (downsample): Sequential(
      (0): Conv2d(256, 512, kernel_size=(1, 1), stride=(2, 2),
      bias=False)
      (1): BatchNorm2d(512, eps=1e-05, momentum=0.1, affine=True,
      track_running_stats=True)
```

```
      )
    )
    (1): BasicBlock(
      (conv1): Conv2d(512, 512, kernel_size=(3, 3), stride=(1, 1),
       padding=(1, 1), bias=False)
      (bn1): BatchNorm2d(512, eps=1e-05, momentum=0.1, affine=True,
       track_running_stats=True)
      (relu): ReLU(inplace)
      (conv2): Conv2d(512, 512, kernel_size=(3, 3), stride=(1, 1),
       padding=(1, 1), bias=False)
      (bn2): BatchNorm2d(512, eps=1e-05, momentum=0.1, affine=True,
       track_running_stats=True)
    )
  )
  (avgpool): AdaptiveAvgPool2d(output_size=(1, 1))
  (fc): Linear(in_features=512, out_features=1000, bias=True)
)
```

There's almost nothing here you haven't already seen in this chapter, with the exception of BatchNorm2d. Let's have a look at what that does in one of those layers.

BatchNorm

BatchNorm, short for *batch normalization,* is a simple layer that has one task in life: using two learned parameters (meaning that it will be trained along with the rest of the network) to try to ensure that each minibatch that goes through the network has a mean centered around zero with a variance of 1. You might ask why we need to do this when we've already normalized our input by using the transform chain in Chapter 2. For smaller networks, BatchNorm is indeed less useful, but as they get larger, the effect of any layer on another, say 20 layers down, can be vast because of repeated multiplication, and you may end up with either vanishing or exploding gradients, both of which are fatal to the training process. The BatchNorm layers make sure that even if you use a model such as ResNet-152, the multiplications inside your network don't get out of hand.

You might be wondering: if we have BatchNorm in our network, why are we normalizing the input at all in the training loop's transformation chain? After all, shouldn't BatchNorm do the work for us? And the answer here is yes, you could do that! But it'll take longer for the network to learn how to get the inputs under control, as they'll have to discover the initial transform themselves, which will make training longer.

I recommend that you instantiate all of the architectures we've talked about so far and use print(model) to see which layers they use and in what order operations happen. After that, there's another key question: *which of these architectures should I use?*

Which Model Should You Use?

The unhelpful answer is, whichever one works best for you, naturally! But let's dig in a little. First, although I suggest that you try the NASNet and PNAS architectures at the moment, I wouldn't wholeheartedly recommend them, despite their impressive results on ImageNet. They can be surprisingly memory-hungry in operation, and the *transfer learning* technique, which you learn about in Chapter 4, is not quite as effective compared to the human-built architectures including ResNet.

I suggest that you have a look around the image-based competitions on Kaggle (*https://www.kaggle.com*), a website that runs hundreds of data science competitions, and see what the winning entries are using. More than likely you'll end up seeing a bunch of ResNet-based ensembles. Personally, I like and use the ResNet architectures over and above any of the others listed here, first because they offer good accuracy, and second because it's easy to start out experimenting with a ResNet-34 model for fast iteration and then move to larger ResNets (and more realistically, an ensemble of different ResNet architectures, just as Microsoft used in their ImageNet win in 2015) once I feel I have something promising.

Before we end the chapter, I have some breaking news concerning downloading pretrained models.

One-Stop Shopping for Models: PyTorch Hub

A recent announcement in the PyTorch world provides an additional route to get models: *PyTorch Hub*. This is supposed to become a central location for obtaining any published model in the future, whether it's for operating on images, text, audio, video, or any other type of data. To obtain a model in this fashion, you use the `torch.hub` module:

```
model = torch.hub.load('pytorch/vision', 'resnet50', pretrained=True)
```

The first parameter points to a GitHub owner and repository (with an optional *tag/branch* identifier in the string as well); the second is the model requested (in this case, `resnet50`); and finally, the third indicates whether to download pretrained weights. You can also use `torch.hub.list('pytorch/vision')` to discover all the models inside that repository that are available to download.

PyTorch Hub is brand new as of mid-2019, so there aren't a huge number of models available as I write this, but I expect it to become a popular way to distribute and download models by the end of the year. All the models in this chapter can be loaded through the `pytorch/vision` repo in PytorchHub, so feel free to use this loading process instead of `torchvision.models`.

Conclusion

In this chapter, you've taken a quick walk-through of how CNN-based neural networks work, including features such as `Dropout`, `MaxPool`, and `BatchNorm`. You've also looked at the most popular architectures used in industry today. Before moving on to the next chapter, play with the architectures we've been talking about and see how they compare. (Don't forget, you don't need to train them! Just download the weights and test the model.)

We're going to close out our look at computer vision by using these pretrained models as a starting point for a custom solution for our cats versus fish problem that uses *transfer learning*.

Further Reading

- AlexNet: "ImageNet Classification with Deep Convolutional Neural Networks" (*https://oreil.ly/CsoFv*) by Alex Krizhevsky et al. (2012)

- VGG: "Very Deep Convolutional Networks for Large-Scale Image Recognition" (*https://arxiv.org/abs/1409.1556*) by Karen Simonyan and Andrew Zisserman (2014)

- Inception: "Going Deeper with Convolutions" (*https://arxiv.org/abs/1409.4842*) by Christian Szegedy et al. (2014)

- ResNet: "Deep Residual Learning for Image Recognition" (*https://arxiv.org/abs/1512.03385*) by Kaiming He et al. (2015)

- NASNet: "Learning Transferable Architectures for Scalable Image Recognition" (*https://arxiv.org/abs/1707.07012*) by Barret Zoph et al. (2017)

CHAPTER 4

Transfer Learning and Other Tricks

Having looked over the architectures in the previous chapter, you might wonder whether you could download an already trained model and train it even further. And the answer is yes! It's an incredibly powerful technique in deep learning circles called *transfer learning*, whereby a network trained for one task (e.g., ImageNet) is adapted to another (fish versus cats).

Why would you do this? It turns out that an architecture trained on ImageNet already knows an awful lot about images, and in particular, quite a bit about whether something is a cat or a fish (or a dog or a whale). Because you're no longer starting from an essentially blank neural network, with transfer learning you're likely to spend much less time in training, *and* you can get away with a vastly smaller training dataset. Traditional deep learning approaches take huge amounts of data to generate good results. With transfer learning, you can build human-level classifiers with a few hundred images.

Transfer Learning with ResNet

Now, the obvious thing to do is to create a ResNet model as we did in Chapter 3 and just slot it into our existing training loop. And you can do that! There's nothing magical in the ResNet model; it's built up from the same building blocks that you've already seen. However, it's a big model, and although you will see some improvement over a baseline ResNet with your data, you will need a lot of data to make sure that the training *signal* gets to all parts of the architecture and trains them significantly toward your new classification task. We're trying to avoid using a lot of data in this approach.

Here's the thing, though: we're not dealing with an architecture that has been initialized with random parameters, as we have done in the past. Our pretrained ResNet model already has a bunch of information encoded into it for image recognition and classification needs, so why bother attempting to retrain it? Instead, we *fine-tune* the network. We alter the architecture slightly to include a new network block at the end, replacing the standard 1,000-category linear layers that normally perform ImageNet classification. We then *freeze* all the existing ResNet layers, and when we train, we update only the parameters in our new layers, but still take the activations from our frozen layers. This allows us to quickly train our new layers while preserving the information that the pretrained layers already contain.

First, let's create a pretrained ResNet-50 model:

```
from torchvision import models
transfer_model = models.ResNet50(pretrained=True)
```

Next, we need to freeze the layers. The way we do this is simple: we stop them from accumulating gradients by using `requires_grad()`. We need to do this for every parameter in the network, but helpfully, PyTorch provides a `parameters()` method that makes this rather easy:

```
for name, param in transfer_model.named_parameters():
    param.requires_grad = False
```

 You might not want to freeze the `BatchNorm` layers in a model, as they will be trained to approximate the mean and standard deviation of the dataset that the model was originally trained on, not the dataset that you want to fine-tune on. Some of the *signal* from your data may end up being lost as `BatchNorm` *corrects* your input. You can look at the model structure and freeze only layers that aren't `BatchNorm` like this:

```
for name, param in transfer_model.named_parameters():
    if("bn" not in name):
        param.requires_grad = False
```

Then we need to replace the final classification block with a new one that we will train for detecting cats or fish. In this example, we replace it with a couple of `Linear` layers, a `ReLU`, and `Dropout`, but you could have extra CNN layers here too. Happily, the definition of PyTorch's implementation of ResNet stores the final classifier block as an instance variable, `fc`, so all we need to do is replace that with our new structure (other models supplied with PyTorch use either `fc` or `classifier`, so you'll probably want to check the definition in the source if you're trying this with a different model type):

```
transfer_model.fc = nn.Sequential(nn.Linear(transfer_model.fc.in_features,500),
nn.ReLU(),
nn.Dropout(), nn.Linear(500,2))
```

In the preceding code, we take advantage of the `in_features` variable that allows us to grab the number of activations coming into a layer (2,048 in this case). You can also use `out_features` to discover the activations coming out. These are handy functions for when you're snapping together networks like building bricks; if the incoming features on a layer don't match the outgoing features of the previous layer, you'll get an error at runtime.

Finally, we go back to our training loop and then train the model as per usual. You should see some large jumps in accuracy even within a few epochs.

Transfer learning is a key technique for improving the accuracy of your deep learning application, but we can employ a bunch of other tricks in order to boost the performance of our model. Let's take a look at some of them.

Finding That Learning Rate

You might remember from Chapter 2 that I introduced the concept of a *learning rate* for training neural networks, mentioned that it was one of the most important hyperparameters you can alter, and then waved away what you should use for it, suggesting a rather small number and for you to experiment with different values. Well…the bad news is, that really is how a lot of people discover the optimum learning rate for their architectures, usually with a technique called *grid search*, exhaustively searching their way through a subset of learning rate values, comparing the results against a validation dataset. This is incredibly time-consuming, and although people do it, many others err on the side of the practioner's lore. For example, a learning rate value that has empirically been observed to work with the Adam optimizer is 3e-4. This is known as Karpathy's constant, after Andrej Karpathy (currently director of AI at Tesla) tweeted about it (*https://oreil.ly/WLw3q*) in 2016. Unfortunately, fewer people read his next tweet: "I just wanted to make sure that people understand that this is a joke." The funny thing is that 3e-4 tends to be a value that can often provide good results, so it's a joke with a hint of reality about it.

On the one hand, you have slow and cumbersome searching, and on the other, obscure and arcane knowledge gained from working on countless architectures until you get a *feel* for what a good learning rate would be—artisanal neural networks, even. Is there a better way than these two extremes?

Thankfully, the answer is yes, although you'll be surprised by how many people don't use this better method. A somewhat obscure paper by Leslie Smith, a research scientist at the US Naval Research Laboratory, contained an approach for finding an appropriate learning rate.[1] But it wasn't until Jeremy Howard brought the technique

---

[1] See "Cyclical Learning Rates for Training Neural Networks" (*https://arxiv.org/abs/1506.01186*) by Leslie Smith (2015).

to the fore in his fast.ai course that it started to catch on in the deep learning community. The idea is quite simple: over the course of an epoch, start out with a small learning rate and increase to a higher learning rate over each mini-batch, resulting in a high rate at the end of the epoch. Calculate the loss for each rate and then, looking at a plot, pick the learning rate that gives the greatest decline. For example, look at the graph in Figure 4-1.

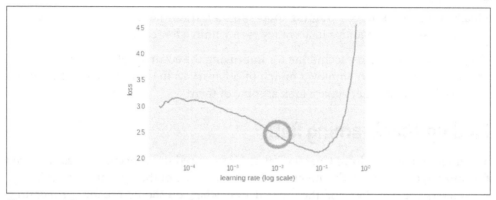

Figure 4-1. Learning rate against loss

In this case, we should look at using a learning rate of around 1e-2 (marked within the circle), as that is roughly the point where the gradient of the descent is steepest.

 Note that you're not looking for the bottom of the curve, which might be the more intuitive place; you're looking for the point that is getting to the bottom the fastest.

Here's a simplified version of what the fast.ai library does under the covers:

```
import math
def find_lr(model, loss_fn, optimizer, init_value=1e-8, final_value=10.0):
    number_in_epoch = len(train_loader) - 1
    update_step = (final_value / init_value) ** (1 / number_in_epoch)
    lr = init_value
    optimizer.param_groups[0]["lr"] = lr
    best_loss = 0.0
    batch_num = 0
    losses = []
    log_lrs = []
    for data in train_loader:
        batch_num += 1
        inputs, labels = data
        inputs, labels = inputs, labels
        optimizer.zero_grad()
        outputs = model(inputs)
```

```
        loss = loss_fn(outputs, labels)

        # Crash out if loss explodes

        if batch_num > 1 and loss > 4 * best_loss:
            return log_lrs[10:-5], losses[10:-5]

        # Record the best loss

        if loss < best_loss or batch_num == 1:
            best_loss = loss

        # Store the values

        losses.append(loss)
        log_lrs.append(math.log10(lr))

        # Do the backward pass and optimize

        loss.backward()
        optimizer.step()

        # Update the lr for the next step and store

        lr *= update_step
        optimizer.param_groups[0]["lr"] = lr
    return log_lrs[10:-5], losses[10:-5]
```

What's going on here is that we iterate through the batches, training almost as usual;
we pass our inputs through the model and then we get the loss from that batch. We
record what our best_loss is so far, and compare the new loss against it. If our new
loss is more than four times the best_loss, we crash out of the function, returning
what we have so far (as the loss is probably tending to infinity). Otherwise, we keep
appending the loss and logs of the current learning rate, and update the learning rate
with the next step along the way to the maximal rate at the end of the loop. The plot
can then be shown using the matplotlib plt function:

```
logs,losses = find_lr()
plt.plot(logs,losses)
found_lr = 1e-2
```

Note that we return slices of the lr logs and losses. We do that simply because the
first bits of training and the last few (especially if the learning rate becomes very large
quite quickly) tend not to tell us much information.

The implementation in fast.ai's library also includes weighted smoothing, so you get
smooth lines in your plot, whereas this snippet produces spiky output. Finally,
remember that because this function does actually train the model and messes with
the optimizer's learning rate settings, you should save and reload your model beforehand to get back to the state it was in before you called find_lr() and also

reinitialize the optimizer you've chosen, which you can do now, passing in the learning rate you've determined from looking at the graph!

That gets us a good value for our learning rate, but we can do even better with *differential learning rates*.

Differential Learning Rates

In our training so far, we have applied one learning rate to the entire model. When training a model from scratch, that probably makes sense, but when it comes to transfer learning, we can normally get a little better accuracy if we try something different: training different groups of layers at different rates. Earlier in the chapter, we froze all the pretrained layers in our model and trained just our new classifier, but we may want to fine-tune some of the layers of, say, the ResNet model we're using. Perhaps adding some training to the layers just preceding our classifier will make our model just a little more accurate. But as those preceding layers have already been trained on the ImageNet dataset, maybe they need only a little bit of training as compared to our newer layers? PyTorch offers a simple way of making this happen. Let's modify our optimizer for the ResNet-50 model:

```
optimizer = optimizer.Adam([
{ 'params': transfer_model.layer4.parameters(), 'lr': found_lr /3},
{ 'params': transfer_model.layer3.parameters(), 'lr': found_lr /9},
], lr=found_lr)
```

That sets the learning rate for `layer4` (just before our classifier) to a third of the *found* learning rate and a ninth for `layer3`. That combination has empirically worked out quite well in my work, but obviously feel free to experiment. There's one more thing, though. As you may remember from the beginning of this chapter, we *froze* all these pretrained layers. It's all very well to give them a different learning rate, but as of right now, the model training won't touch them at all because they don't accumulate gradients. Let's change that:

```
unfreeze_layers = [transfer_model.layer3, transfer_model.layer4]
for layer in unfreeze_layers:
    for param in layer.parameters():
        param.requires_grad = True
```

Now that the parameters in these layers take gradients once more, the differential learning rates will be applied when you fine-tine the model. Note that you can freeze and unfreeze parts of the model at will and do further fine-tuning on every layer separately if you'd like!

Now that we've looked at the learning rates, let's investigate a different aspect of training our models: the data that we feed into them.

Data Augmentation

One of the dreaded phrases in data science is, *Oh no, my model has overfit on the data!* As I mentioned in Chapter 2, *overfitting* occurs when the model decides to reflect the data presented in the training set rather than produce a generalized solution. You'll often hear people talking about how a particular model *memorized the dataset*, meaning the model learned the answers and went on to perform poorly on production data.

The traditional way of guarding against this is to amass large quantities of data. By seeing more data, the model gets a more general idea of the problem it is trying to solve. If you view the situation as a compression problem, then if you prevent the model from simply being able to store all the answers (by overwhelming its storage capacity with so much data), it's forced to *compress* the input and therefore produce a solution that cannot simply be storing the answers within itself. This is fine, and works well, but say we have only a thousand images and we're doing transfer learning. What can we do?

One approach that we can use is *data augmentation*. If we have an image, we can do a number of things to that image that should prevent overfitting and make the model more general. Consider the images of Helvetica the cat in Figures 4-2 and 4-3.

Figure 4-2. Our original image

Figure 4-3. A flipped Helvetica

Obviously to us, they're the same image. The second one is just a mirrored copy of the first. The tensor representation is going to be different, as the RGB values will be in different places in the 3D image. But it's still a cat, so the model training on this image will hopefully learn to recognize a cat shape on the left or right side of the frame, rather than simply associating the entire image with *cat*. Doing this in PyTorch is simple. You may remember this snippet of code from Chapter 2:

```
transforms = transforms.Compose([
        transforms.Resize(64),
        transforms.ToTensor(),
        transforms.Normalize(mean=[0.485, 0.456, 0.406],
                std=[0.229, 0.224, 0.225] )
        ])
```

This forms a transformation pipeline that all images go through as they enter the model for training. But the `torchvision.transforms` library contains many other transformation functions that can be used to augment training data. Let's have a look at some of the more useful ones and see what happens to Helvetica with some of the less obvious transforms as well.

Torchvision Transforms

`torchvision` comes complete with a large collection of potential transforms that can be used for data augmentation, plus two ways of constructing new transformations. In this section, we look at the most useful ones that come supplied as well as a couple of custom transformations that you can use in your own applications.

```
torchvision.transforms.ColorJitter(brightness=0, contrast=0, saturation=0, hue=0)
```

`ColorJitter` randomly changes the brightness, contrast, saturation, and hue of an image. For brightness, contrast, and saturation, you can supply either a float or a tuple of floats, all nonnegative in the range 0 to 1, and the randomness will either be between 0 and the supplied float or it will use the tuple to generate randomness between the supplied pair of floats. For hue, a float or float tuple between −0.5 and 0.5 is required, and it will generate random hue adjustments between [*-hue,hue*] or [*min, max*]. See Figure 4-4 for an example.

Figure 4-4. ColorJitter applied at 0.5 for all parameters

If you want to flip your image, these two transforms randomly reflect an image on either the horizontal or vertical axis:

```
torchvision.transforms.RandomHorizontalFlip(p=0.5)
torchvision.transforms.RandomVerticalFlip(p=0.5)
```

Either supply a float from 0 to 1 for the probability of the reflection to occur or accept the default of a 50% chance of reflection. A vertically flipped cat is shown in Figure 4-5.

Figure 4-5. Vertical flip

RandomGrayscale is a similar type of transformation, except that it randomly turns the image grayscale, depending on the parameter *p* (the default is 10%):

```
torchvision.transforms.RandomGrayscale(p=0.1)
```

`RandomCrop` and `RandomResizeCrop`, as you might expect, perform random crops on the image of `size`, which can either be an int for height and width, or a tuple containing different heights and widths. Figure 4-6 shows an example of a `RandomCrop` in action.

```
torchvision.transforms.RandomCrop(size, padding=None,
pad_if_needed=False, fill=0, padding_mode='constant')
torchvision.transforms.RandomResizedCrop(size, scale=(0.08, 1.0),
ratio=(0.75, 1.3333333333333333), interpolation=2)
```

Now you need to be a little careful here, because if your crops are too small, you run the risk of cutting out important parts of the image and making the model train on the wrong thing. For instance, if a cat is playing on a table in an image, and the crop takes out the cat and just leaves part of the table to be classified as *cat*, that's not great. While the `RandomResizeCrop` will resize the crop to fill the given size, `RandomCrop` may take a crop close to the edge and into the darkness beyond the image.

> `RandomResizeCrop` is using Bilinear interpolation, but you can also select nearest neighbor or bicubic interpolation by changing the `interpolation` parameter. See the PIL filters page (*https://oreil.ly/rNOtN*) for further details.

As you saw in Chapter 3, we can add padding to maintain the required size of the image. By default, this is `constant` padding, which fills out the otherwise empty pixels beyond the image with the value given in `fill`. However, I recommend that you use the `reflect` padding instead, as empirically it seems to work a little better than just throwing in empty constant space.

Figure 4-6. RandomCrop with size=100

If you'd like to randomly rotate an image, `RandomRotation` will vary between [-degrees, degrees] if `degrees` is a single float or int, or (min,max) if it is a tuple:

```
torchvision.transforms.RandomRotation(degrees, resample=False,expand=False, center=None)
```

If `expand` is set to `True`, this function will expand the output image so that it can include the entire rotation; by default, it's set to crop to within the input dimensions. You can specify a PIL resampling filter, and optionally provide an (x,y) tuple for the center of rotation; otherwise the transform will rotate about the center of the image. Figure 4-7 is a RandomRotation transformation with degrees set to 45.

Figure 4-7. RandomRotation with degrees = 45

Pad is a general-purpose padding transform that adds padding (extra height and width) onto the borders of an image:

```
torchvision.transforms.Pad(padding, fill=0, padding_mode=constant)
```

A single value in padding will apply padding on that length in all directions. A two-tuple padding will produce padding in the length of (left/right, top/bottom), and a four-tuple will produce padding for (left, top, right, bottom). By default, padding is set to constant mode, which copies the value of fill into the padding slots. The other choices are edge, which pads the last values of the edge of the image into the padding length; reflect, which reflects the values of the image (except the edge) into the border; and symmetric, which is reflection but includes the last value of the image at the edge. Figure 4-8 shows padding set to 25 and padding_mode set to reflect. See how the box repeats at the edges.

Figure 4-8. Pad with padding = 25 and padding_mode = reflect

`RandomAffine` allows you to specify random affine translations of the image (scaling, rotations, translations, and/or shearing, or any combination). Figure 4-9 shows an example of an affine transformation.

```
torchvision.transforms.RandomAffine(degrees, translate=None, scale=None,
shear=None, resample=False, fillcolor=0)
```

Figure 4-9. RandomAffine with degrees = 10 and shear = 50

The `degrees` parameter is either a single float or int or a tuple. In single form, it produces random rotations between (*–degrees, degrees*). With a tuple, it will produce random rotations between (*min, max*). `degrees` has to be explicitly set to prevent rotations from occurring—there's no default setting. `translate` is a tuple of two multipliers (*horizontal_multipler, vertical_multiplier*). At transform time, a horizontal shift, dx, is sampled in the range *–image_width × horizontal_multiplier < dx <*

img_width × horizontal_width, and a vertical shift is sampled in the same way with respect to the image height and the vertical multiplier.

Scaling is handled by another tuple, (*min, max*), and a uniform scaling factor is randomly sampled from those. Shearing can be either a single float/int or a tuple, and randomly samples in the same manner as the degrees parameter. Finally, resample allows you to optionally provide a PIL resampling filter, and fillcolor is an optional int specifying a fill color for areas inside the final image that lie outside the final transform.

As for what transforms you should use in a data augmentation pipeline, I definitely recommend using the various random flips, color jittering, rotation, and crops to start.

Other transformations are available in torchvision; check the documentation (*https://oreil.ly/b0Q0A*) for more details. But of course you may find yourself wanting to create a transformation that is particular to your data domain that isn't included by default, so PyTorch provides various ways of defining custom transformations, as you'll see next.

Color Spaces and Lambda Transforms

This may seem a little odd to even bring up, but so far all our image work has been in the fairly standard 24-bit RGB color space, where every pixel has an 8-bit red, green, and blue value to indicate the color of that pixel. However, other color spaces are available!

A popular alternative is HSV, which has three 8-bit values for *hue, saturation*, and *value*. Some people feel this system more accurately models human vision than the traditional RGB color space. But why does this matter? A mountain in RGB is a mountain in HSV, right?

Well, there's some evidence from recent deep learning work in colorization that other color spaces can produce slightly higher accuracy than RGB. A mountain may be a mountain, but the tensor that gets formed in each space's representation will be different, and one space may capture something about your data better than another.

When combined with ensembles, you could easily create a series of models that combines the results of training on RGB, HSV, YUV, and LAB color spaces to wring out a few more percentage points of accuracy from your prediction pipeline.

One slight problem is that PyTorch doesn't offer a transform that can do this. But it does provide a couple of tools that we can use to randomly change an image from standard RGB into HSV (or another color space). First, if we look in the PIL documentation, we see that we can use Image.convert() to translate a PIL image from one color space to another. We could write a custom transform class to carry out this conversion, but PyTorch adds a `transforms.Lambda` class so that we can easily wrap any function and make it available to the transform pipeline. Here's our custom function:

```
def _random_colour_space(x):
    output = x.convert("HSV")
    return output
```

This is then wrapped in a `transforms.Lambda` class and can be used in any standard transformation pipeline like we've seen before:

```
colour_transform = transforms.Lambda(lambda x: _random_colour_space(x))
```

That's fine if we want to convert *every* image into HSV, but really we don't want that. We'd like it to randomly change images in each batch, so it's probable that the image will be presented in different color spaces in different epochs. We could update our original function to generate a random number and use that to generate a random probability of changing the image, but instead we're even lazier and use `RandomApply`:

```
random_colour_transform = torchvision.transforms.RandomApply([colour_transform])
```

By default, `RandomApply` fills in a parameter `p` with a value of `0.5`, so there's a 50/50 chance of the transform being applied. Experiment with adding more color spaces and the probability of applying the transformation to see what effect it has on our cat and fish problem.

Let's look at another custom transform that is a little more complicated.

Custom Transform Classes

Sometimes a simple lambda isn't enough; maybe we have some initialization or state that we want to keep track of, for example. In these cases, we can create a custom transform that operates on either PIL image data or a tensor. Such a class has to implement two methods: `__call__`, which the transform pipeline will invoke during the transformation process; and `__repr__`, which should return a string representation of the transform, along with any state that may be useful for diagnostic purposes.

In the following code, we implement a transform class that adds random Gaussian noise to a tensor. When the class is initialized, we pass in the mean and standard distribution of the noise we require, and during the `__call__` method, we sample from this distribution and add it to the incoming tensor:

```
class Noise():
    """Adds gaussian noise to a tensor.

    >>> transforms.Compose([
    >>>     transforms.ToTensor(),
    >>>     Noise(0.1, 0.05)),
    >>> ])
```

```
"""
    def __init__(self, mean, stddev):
        self.mean = mean
        self.stddev = stddev

    def __call__(self, tensor):
        noise = torch.zeros_like(tensor).normal_(self.mean, self.stddev)
        return tensor.add_(noise)

    def __repr__(self):
        repr = f"{self.__class__.__name__ }(mean={self.mean},
            stddev={self.stddev})"
        return repr
```

If we add this to a pipeline, we can see the results of the __repr__ method being called:

```
transforms.Compose([Noise(0.1, 0.05))])
>> Compose(
    Noise(mean=0.1,sttdev=0.05)
)
```

Because transforms don't have any restrictions and just inherit from the base Python object class, you can do anything. Want to completely replace an image at runtime with something from Google image search? Run the image through a completely different neural network and pass that result down the pipeline? Apply a series of image transforms that turn the image into a crazed reflective shadow of its former self? All possible, if not entirely recommended. Although it would be interesting to see whether Photoshop's *Twirl* transformation effect would make accuracy worse or better! Why not give it a go?

Aside from transformations, there are a few more ways of squeezing as much performance from a model as possible. Let's look at more examples.

Start Small and Get Bigger!

Here's a tip that seems odd, but obtains real results: start small and get bigger. What I mean is if you're training on 256 × 256 images, create a few more datasets in which the images have been scaled to 64 × 64 and 128 × 128. Create your model with the 64 × 64 dataset, fine-tune as normal, and then train the *exact same model* with the 128 × 128 dataset. Not from scratch, but using the parameters that have already been trained. Once it looks like you've squeezed the most out of the 128 × 128 data, move on to your target 256 × 256 data. You'll probably find a percentage point or two improvement in accuracy.

While we don't know exactly why this works, the working theory is that by training at the lower resolutions, the model learns about the overall structure of the image and can refine that knowledge as the incoming images expand. But that's just a theory.

However, that doesn't stop it from being a good little trick to have up your sleeve when you need to squeeze every last bit of performance from a model.

If you don't want to have multiple copies of a dataset hanging around in storage, you can use `torchvision` transforms to do this on the fly using the `Resize` function:

```
resize = transforms.Compose([ transforms.Resize(64),
…_other augmentation transforms_…
transforms.ToTensor(),
transforms.Normalize([0.485, 0.456, 0.406], [0.229, 0.224, 0.225])
```

The penalty you pay here is that you end up spending more time in training, as PyTorch has to apply the resize every time. If you resized all the images beforehand, you'd likely get a quicker training run, at the expense of filling up your hard drive. But isn't that trade-off always the way?

The concept of starting small and then getting bigger also applies to architectures. Using a ResNet architecture like ResNet-18 or ResNet-34 to test out approaches to transforms and get a feel for how training is working provides a much tighter feedback loop than if you start out using a ResNet-101 or ResNet-152 model. Start small, build upward, and you can potentially reuse the smaller model runs at prediction time by adding them to an ensemble model.

Ensembles

What's better than one model making predictions? Well, how about a bunch of them? *Ensembling* is a technique that is fairly common in more traditional machine learning methods, and it works rather well in deep learning too. The idea is to obtain a prediction from a series of models, and combine those predictions to produce a final answer. Because different models will have different strengths in different areas, hopefully a combination of all their predictions will produce a more accurate result than one model alone.

There are plenty of approaches to ensembles, and we won't go into all of them here. Instead, here's a simple way of getting started with ensembles, one that has eeked out another 1% of accuracy in my experience; simply average the predictions:

```
# Assuming you have a list of models in models, and input is your input tensor

predictions = [m[i].fit(input) for i in models]
avg_prediction = torch.stack(b).mean(0).argmax()
```

The `stack` method concatenates the array of tensors together, so if we were working on the cat/fish problem and had four models in our ensemble, we'd end up with a 4 × 2 tensor constructed from the four 1 × 2 tensors. And `mean` does what you'd expect, taking the average, although we have to pass in a dimension of 0 to ensure that it takes an average across the first dimension instead of simply adding up all the tensor elements and producing a scalar output. Finally, `argmax` picks out the tensor index with the highest element, as you've seen before.

It's easy to imagine more complex approaches. Perhaps weights could be added to each individual model's prediction, and those weights adjusted if a model gets an answer right or wrong. What models should you use? I've found that a combination of ResNets (e.g., 34, 50, 101) work quite well, and there's nothing to stop you from saving your model regularly and using different snapshots of the model across time in your ensemble!

Conclusion

As we come to the end of Chapter 4, we're leaving images behind to move on to text. Hopefully you not only understand how convolutional neural networks work on images, but also have a deep bag of tricks in hand, including transfer learning, learning rate finding, data augmentation, and ensembling, which you can bring to bear on your particular application domain.

Further Reading

If you're interested in learning more in the image realm, check out the fast.ai (*https:// fast.ai*) course by Jeremy Howard, Rachel Thomas, and Sylvain Gugger. This chapter's learning rate finder is, as I mentioned, a simplified version of the one they use, but the course goes into further detail about many of the techniques in this chapter. The fast.ai library, built on PyTorch, allows you to bring them to bear on your image (and text!) domains easily.

- Torchvision documentation (*https://oreil.ly/vNnST*)
- PIL/Pillow documentation (*https://oreil.ly/Jlisb*)
- "Cyclical Learning Rates for Training Neural Networks" (*https://arxiv.org/abs/1506.01186*) by Leslie N. Smith (2015)
- "ColorNet: Investigating the Importance of Color Spaces for Image Classification" (*https://arxiv.org/abs/1902.00267*) by Shreyank N. Gowda and Chun Yuan (2019)

CHAPTER 5

Text Classification

We're leaving images behind for now and turning our attention to another area where deep learning has proven to be a significant advance on traditional techniques: *natural language processing (NLP)*. A good example of this is Google Translate. Originally, the code that handled translation was a weighty 500,000 lines of code. The new, TensorFlow-based system has approximately 500, and it performs better than the old method.

Recent breakthroughs also have occurred in bringing transfer learning (which you learned about in Chapter 4) to NLP problems. New architectures such as the Transformer architecture have led to the creation of networks like OpenAI's GPT-2, the larger variant of which produces text that is almost human-like in quality (and in fact, OpenAI has not released the weights of this model for fear of it being used maliciously).

This chapter provides a whirlwind tour of recurrent neural networks and embeddings. Then we explore the `torchtext` library and how to use it for text processing with an LSTM-based model.

Recurrent Neural Networks

If we look back at how we've been using our CNN-based architectures so far, we can see they have always been working on one complete snapshot of time. But consider these two sentence fragments:

```
The cat sat on the mat.
```

```
She got up and impatiently climbed on the chair, meowing for food.
```

Say you were to feed those two sentences, one after the other, into a CNN and ask, *where is the cat?* You'd have a problem, because the network has no concept of *memory.* This is incredibly important when it comes to dealing with data that has a temporal domain (e.g., text, speech, video, and time-series data).[1] *Recurrent neural networks* (RNNs) answer this problem by giving neural networks a memory via *hidden state.*

What does an RNN look like? My favorite explanation is, "Imagine a neural network crossed with a `for` loop." Figure 5-1 shows a diagram of a classical RNN structure.

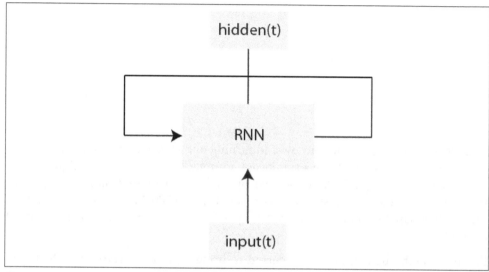

Figure 5-1. An RNN

We add input at a time step of *t*, and we get a *hidden* output state of *ht*, and the output also gets fed back into the RNN for the next time step. We can unroll this network to take a deeper look at what's going on, as shown in Figure 5-2.

---

1 Note that it's not impossible to do these things with CNNs; a lot of in-depth research in the last few years has been done to apply CNN-based networks in the temporal domain. We won't cover them here, but "Temporal Convolutional Networks: A Unified Approach to Action Segmentation" (*https://arxiv.org/abs/1608.08242*) by Colin Lea, et al. (2016) provides further information. And seq2seq!

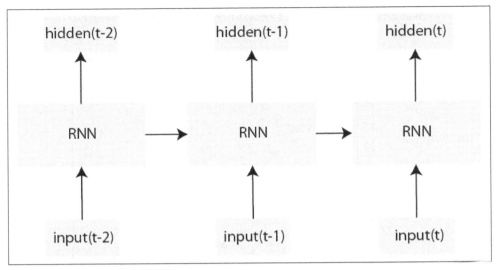

Figure 5-2. An unrolled RNN

What we have here is a grouping of fully connected layers (with shared parameters), a series of inputs, and our output. Input data is fed into the network, and the next item in the sequence is predicted as output. In the unrolled view, we can see that the RNN can be thought of as a pipeline of fully connected layers, with the successive input being fed into the next layer in the sequence (with the usual nonlinearities such as ReLU being inserted between the layers). When we have our completed predicted sequence, we then have to backpropagate the error back through the RNN. Because this involves stepping back through the network's steps, this process is known as backpropagation through time. The error is calculated on the entire sequence, then the network is unfolded as in Figure 5-2, and the gradients are calculated for each time step and combined to update the shared parameters of the network. You can imagine it as doing backprop on individual networks and summing all the gradients together.

That's the theory behind RNNs. But this simple structure has problems that we need to talk about and how they were overcome with newer architectures.

Long Short-Term Memory Networks

In practice, RNNs were and are particularly susceptible to the *vanishing gradient* problem we talked about in Chapter 2, or the potentially worse scenario of the *exploding gradient*, where your error tends off toward infinity. Neither is good, so RNNs couldn't be brought to bear on many of the problems they were considered suitable for. That all changed in 1997 when Sepp Hochreiter and Jürgen Schmidhuber introduced the Long Short-Term Memory (LSTM) variant of the RNN.

Figure 5-3 diagrams an LSTM layer. I know, there's a lot going on here, but it's not too complex. Honest.

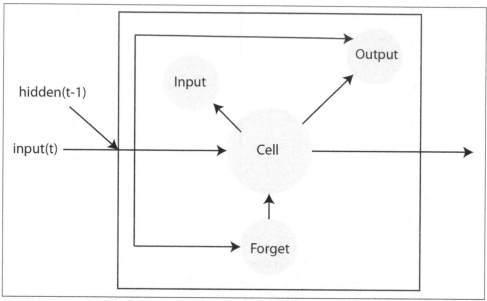

Figure 5-3. An LSTM

OK, I admit, it is quite intimidating. The key is to think about the three gates (input, output, and forget). In a standard RNN, we "remember" everything forever. But that's not how our brains work (sadly!), and the LSTM's forget gate allows us to model the idea that as we continue in our input chain, the beginning of the chain becomes less important. And how much the LSTM forgets is something that is learned during training, so if it's in the network's best interest to be very forgetful, the forget gate parameters will do so.

The *cell* ends up being the "memory" of the network layer; and the input, output, and forget gates will determine how data flows through the layer. The data may simply pass through, it may "write" to the cell, and that data may (or may not!) flow through to the next layer, modified by the output gate.

This assemblage of parts was enough to solve the vanishing gradient problem, and also has the virtue of being Turing-complete, so theoretically, you can do any calculation that you can do on a computer with one of these.

But things didn't stop there, of course. Several developments have occurred in the RNN space since LSTMs, and we'll cover some of the major ones in the next sections.

Gated Recurrent Units

Since 1997, many variants of the base LSTM network have been created, most of which you probably don't need to know about unless you're curious. However, one variant that came along in 2014, the gated recurrent unit (GRU), is worth knowing about, as it has become quite popular in some circles. Figure 5-4 shows the makeup of a GRU architecture.

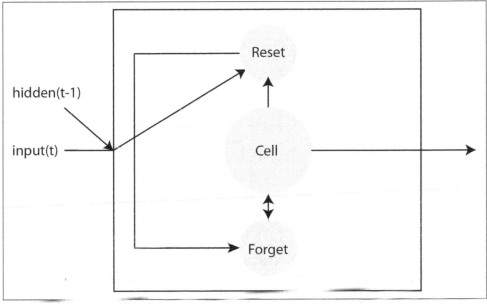

Figure 5-4. A GRU

The main takeaway is that the GRU has merged the forget gate with the output gate. This means that it has fewer parameters than an LSTM and so tends to be quicker to train and uses fewer resources at runtime. For these reasons, and also that they're essentially a drop-in replacement for LSTMs, they've become quite popular. However, strictly speaking, they are less powerful than LSTMs because of the merging of the forget and output gates, so in general I recommend playing with both GRUs or LSTMs in your network and seeing which one performs better. Or just accept that the LSTM may be a little slower in training, but may end up being the best choice in the end. You don't have to follow the latest fad—honest!

biLSTM

Another common variant of the LSTM is the *bidirectional* LSTM or *biLSTM* for short. As you've seen so far, traditional LSTMs (and RNNs in general) can look to the past as they are trained and make decisions. Unfortunately, sometimes you need to see the future as well. This is particularly the case in applications like translation and handwriting recognition, where what comes after the current state can be just as important as the previous state for determining output.

A biLSTM solves this problem in the simplest of ways: it's essentially two stacked LSTMs, with the input being sent in the forward direction in one LSTM and reversed in the second. Figure 5-5 shows how a biLSTM works across its input bidirectionally to produce the output.

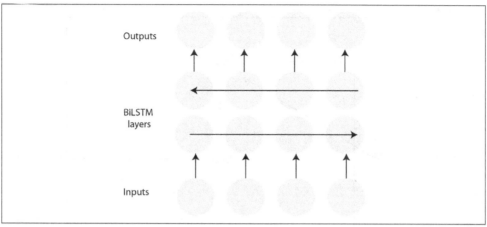

Figure 5-5. A biLSTM

PyTorch makes it easy to create biLSTMs by passing in a `bidirectional=True` parameter when creating an `LSTM()` unit, as you'll see later in the chapter.

That completes our tour throughout the RNN-based architectures. In Chapter 9, we return to the question of architecture when we look at the Transformer-based BERT and GPT-2 models.

Embeddings

We're almost at the point where we can start writing some code! But before we do, one little detail may have occurred to you: how do we represent words in a network? After all, we're feeding tensors of numbers into a network and getting tensors out. With images, it seemed a fairly obvious thing to convert them into tensors representing the red/green/blue component values, and they're already naturally thought of as arrays as they come with a height and width baked in. But words? Sentences? How is that going to work?

The simplest approach is still one that you'll find in many approaches to NLP, and it's called *one-hot encoding*. It's pretty simple! Let's look at our first sentence from the start of the chapter:

```
The cat sat on the mat.
```

If we consider that this is the entire vocabulary of our world, we have a tensor of [the, cat, sat, on, mat]. One-hot encoding simply means that we create a vector that is the size of the vocabulary, and for each word in it, we allocate a vector with one parameter set to 1 and the rest to 0:

```
the - [1 0 0 0 0]
cat - [0 1 0 0 0]
sat - [0 0 1 0 0]
on  - [0 0 0 1 0]
mat - [0 0 0 0 1]
```

We've now converted the words into vectors, and we can feed them into our network. Additionally, we may add extra symbols into our vocabulary, such as UNK (unknown, for words not in the vocabulary) and START/STOP to signify the beginning and ends of sentences.

One-hot encoding has a few limitations that become clearer when we add another word into our example vocabulary: *kitty*. From our encoding scheme, *kitty* would be represented by [0 0 0 0 0 1] (with all the other vectors being padded with a zero). First, you can see that if we are going to model a realistic set of words, our vectors are going to be very long with almost no information in them. Second, and perhaps more importantly, we know that a *very strong* relationship exists between the words *kitty* and *cat* (also with *dammit*, but thankfully that's been skipped from our vocab here!), and this is impossible to represent with one-hot encoding; the two words are completely different things.

An approach that has become more popular recently is replacing one-hot encoding with an *embedding matrix* (of course, a one-hot encoding is an embedding matrix itself, just one that doesn't contain any information about relationships between words). The idea is to squash the dimensionality of the vector space down to something a little more manageable and take advantage of the space itself.

For example, if we have an embedding in a 2D space, perhaps *cat* could be represented by the tensor [0.56, 0.45] and *kitten* by [0.56, 0.445], whereas *mat* could be [0.2, -0.1]. We cluster similar words together in the vector space and can do distance checks such as Euclidean or cosine distance functions to determine how close words are to each other. And how do we determine where words fall in the vector space? An embedding layer is no different from any other layer you've seen so far in building neural networks; we initialize the vector space randomly, and hopefully the training process updates the parameters so that similar words or concepts gravitate toward each other.

A famous example of embedding vectors is *word2vec*, which was released by Google in 2013.[2] This was a set of word embeddings trained using a shallow neural network, and it revealed that the transformation into vector space seemed to capture something about the concepts underpinning the words. In its commonly cited finding, if you pulled the vectors for *King*, *Man*, and *Woman* and then subtracted the vector for *Man* from *King* and added the vector for *Woman*, you would get a result that was the vector representation for *Queen*. Since *word2vec*, other pretrained embeddings have become available, such as *ELMo*, *GloVe*, and *fasttext*.

As for using embeddings in PyTorch, it's really simple:

```
embed = nn.Embedding(vocab_size, dimension_size)
```

This will contain a tensor of `vocab_size` x `dimension_size` initialized randomly. I prefer to think that it's just a giant array or lookup table. Each word in your vocabulary indexes into an entry that is a vector of `dimension_size`, so if we go back to our cat and its epic adventures on the mat, we'd have something like this:

```
cat_mat_embed = nn.Embedding(5, 2)
cat_tensor = Tensor([1])
cat_mat_embed.forward(cat_tensor)

> tensor([[ 1.7793, -0.3127]], grad_fn=<EmbeddingBackward>)
```

We create our embedding, a tensor that contains the position of *cat* in our vocabulary, and pass it through the layer's `forward()` method. That gives us our random embedding. The result also points out that we have a gradient function that we can use for updating the parameters after we combine it with a loss function.

We've now gone through all the theory and can get started on building something!

torchtext

Just like `torchvision`, PyTorch provides an official library, `torchtext`, for handling text-processing pipelines. However, `torchtext` is not quite as battle-tested or has as many eyes on it as `torchvision`, which means it's not quite as easy to use or as well-documented. But it is still a powerful library that can handle a lot of the mundane work of building up text-based datasets, so we'll be using it for the rest of the chapter.

Installing `torchtext` is fairly simple. You use either standard `pip`:

```
pip install torchtext
```

or a specific `conda` channel:

---

2 See "Efficient Estimation of Word Representations in Vector Space" (*https://arxiv.org/abs/1301.3781*) by Tomas Mikolov et al. (2013).

```
conda install -c derickl torchtext
```

You'll also want to install *spaCy* (an NLP library), and pandas if you don't have them on your system (again, either using `pip` or `conda`). We use *spaCy* for processing our text in the `torchtext` pipeline, and pandas for exploring and cleaning up our data.

Getting Our Data: Tweets!

In this section, we build a sentiment analysis model, so let's grab a dataset. `torchtext` provides a bunch of built-in datasets via the `torchtext.datasets` module, but we're going to work on one from scratch to get a feel for building a custom dataset and feeding it into a model we've created. We use the Sentiment140 dataset (*http://help.sentiment140.com/for-students*). This is based on tweets from Twitter, with every tweet ranked as 0 for negative, 2 for neutral, and 4 for positive.

Download the zip archive and unzip. We use the file *training.1600000.processed.noemoticon.csv*. Let's look at the file using pandas:

```
import pandas as pd
tweetsDF = pd.read_csv("training.1600000.processed.noemoticon.csv",
                       header=None)
```

You may at this point get an error like this:

```
UnicodeDecodeError: 'utf-8' codec can't decode bytes in
position 80-81: invalid continuation byte
```

Congratulations—you're now a real data scientist and you get to deal with data cleaning! From the error message, it appears that the default C-based CSV parser that pandas uses doesn't like some of the Unicode in the file, so we need to switch to the Python-based parser:

```
tweetsDF = pd.read_csv("training.1600000.processed.noemoticon.csv",
engine="python", header=None)
```

Let's take a look at the structure of the data by displaying the first five rows:

```
>>> tweetDF.head(5)
0  0  1467810672  ...  NO_QUERY   scotthamilton  is upset that ...
1  0  1467810917  ...  NO_QUERY        mattycus  @Kenichan I dived many times ...
2  0  1467811184  ...  NO_QUERY         ElleCTF   my whole body feels itchy
3  0  1467811193  ...  NO_QUERY          Karoli  @nationwideclass no, it's ...
4  0  1467811372  ...  NO_QUERY        joy_wolf  @Kwesidei not the whole crew
```

Annoyingly, we don't have a header field in this CSV (again, welcome to the world of a data scientist!), but by looking at the website and using our intuition, we can see that what we're interested in is the last column (the tweet text) and the first column (our labeling). However, the labels aren't great, so let's do a little feature engineering to work around that. Let's see what counts we have in our training set:

```
>>> tweetsDF[0].value_counts()
4    800000
0    800000
Name: 0, dtype: int64
```

Curiously, there are no neutral values in the training dataset. This means that we could formulate the problem as a binary choice between 0 and 1 and work out our predictions from there, but for now we stick to the original plan that we may possibly have neutral tweets in the future. To encode the classes as numbers starting from 0, we first create a column of type `category` from the label column:

```
tweetsDF["sentiment_cat"] = tweetsDF[0].astype('category')
```

Then we encode those classes as numerical information in another column:

```
tweetsDF["sentiment"] = tweetsDF["sentiment_cat"].cat.codes
```

We then save the modified CSV back to disk:

```
tweetsDF.to_csv("train-processed.csv", header=None, index=None)
```

I recommend that you save another CSV that has a small sample of the 1.6 million tweets for you to test things out on too:

```
tweetsDF.sample(10000).to_csv("train-processed-sample.csv", header=None,
    index=None)
```

Now we need to tell `torchtext` what we think is important for the purposes of creating a dataset.

Defining Fields

`torchtext` takes a straightforward approach to generating datasets: you tell it what you want, and it'll process the raw CSV (or JSON) for you. You do this by first defining *fields*. The `Field` class has a considerable number of parameters that can be assigned to it, and although you probably won't use all of them at once, Table 5-1 provides a handy guide as to what you can do with a `Field`.

Table 5-1. Field parameter types

Parameter	Description	Default
sequential	Whether the field represents sequential data (i.e., text). If set to `False`, no tokenization is applied.	True
use_vocab	Whether to include a `Vocab` object. If set to `False`, the field should contain numerical data.	True
init_token	A token that will be added to the start of this field to indicate the beginning of the data.	None
eos_token	End-of-sentence token appended to the end of each sequence.	None
fix_length	If set to an integer, all entries will be padded to this length. If None, sequence lengths will be flexible.	None

Parameter	Description	Default
dtype	The type of the tensor batch.	torch.long
lower	Convert the sequence into lowercase.	False
tokenize	The function that will perform sequence tokenization. If set to spaCy, the spaCy tokenizer will be used.	string.split
pad_token	The token that will be used as padding.	<pad>
unk_token	The token that will be used to represent words that are not present in the Vocab dict.	<unk>
pad_first	Pad at the start of the sequence.	False
trun cate_first	Truncate at the beginning of the sequence (if necessary).	False

As we noted, we're interested in only the labels and the tweets text. We define these by using the Field datatype:

```
from torchtext import data

LABEL = data.LabelField()
TWEET = data.Field(tokenize='spacy', lower=true)
```

We're defining LABEL as a LabelField, which is a subclass of Field that sets sequen tial to False (as it's our numerical category class). TWEET is a standard Field object, where we have decided to use the spaCy tokenizer and convert all the text to lower-case, but otherwise we're using the defaults as listed in the previous table. If, when running through this example, the step of building the vocabulary is taking a very long time, try removing the tokenize parameter and rerunning. This will use the default of simply splitting on whitespace, which will speed up the tokenization step considerably, though the created vocabulary will not be as good as the one spaCy creates.

Having defined those fields, we now need to produce a list that maps them onto the list of rows that are in the CSV:

```
fields = [('score',None), ('id',None),('date',None),('query',None),
    ('name',None),
    ('tweet', TWEET),('category',None),('label',LABEL)]
```

Armed with our declared fields, we now use TabularDataset to apply that definition to the CSV:

```
twitterDataset = torchtext.data.TabularDataset(
        path="training-processed.csv",
        format="CSV",
        fields=fields,
        skip_header=False)
```

This may take some time, especially with the spaCy parser. Finally, we can split into training, testing, and validation sets by using the split() method:

```
(train, test, valid) = twitterDataset.split(split_ratio=[0.8,0.1,0.1])

(len(train),len(test),len(valid))
> (1280000, 160000, 160000)
```

Here's an example pulled from the dataset:

```
>vars(train.examples[7])

{'label': '6681',
 'tweet': ['woah',
  ',',
  'hell',
  'in',
  'chapel',
  'thrill',
  'is',
  'closed',
  '.',
  'no',
  'more',
  'sweaty',
  'basement',
  'dance',
  'parties',
  '?',
  '?']}
```

In a surprising turn of serendipity, the randomly selected tweet references the closure of a club in Chapel Hill I frequently visited. See if you find anything as weird on your dive through the data!

Building a Vocabulary

Traditionally, at this point we would build a one-hot encoding of each word that is present in the dataset—a rather tedious process. Thankfully, torchtext will do this for us, and will also allow a max_size parameter to be passed in to limit the vocabulary to the most common words. This is normally done to prevent the construction of a huge, memory-hungry model. We don't want our GPUs too overwhelmed, after all. Let's limit the vocabulary to a maximum of 20,000 words in our training set:

```
vocab_size = 20000
TWEET.build_vocab(train, max_size = vocab_size)
```

We can then interrogate the vocab class instance object to make some discoveries about our dataset. First, we ask the traditional "How big is our vocabulary?":

```
len(TWEET.vocab)
> 20002
```

Wait, *wait, what?* Yes, we specified 20,000, but by default, torchtext will add two more special tokens, <unk> for unknown words (e.g., those that get cut off by the 20,000 max_size we specified), and <pad>, a padding token that will be used to pad all our text to roughly the same size to help with efficient batching on the GPU (remember that a GPU gets its speed from operating on regular batches). You can also specify eos_token or init_token symbols when you declare a field, but they're not included by default.

Now let's take a look at the most common words in the vocabulary:

```
>TWEET.vocab.freqs.most_common(10)
[('!', 44802),
 ('.', 40088),
 ('I', 33133),
 (' ', 29484),
 ('to', 28024),
 ('the', 24389),
 (',', 23951),
 ('a', 18366),
 ('i', 17189),
 ('and', 14252)]
```

Pretty much what you'd expect, as we're not removing stop-words with our spaCy tokenizer. (Because it's just 140 characters, we'd be in danger of losing too much information from our model if we did.)

We are almost finished with our datasets. We just need to create a data loader to feed into our training loop. torchtext provides the BucketIterator method that will produce what it calls a Batch, which is almost, but not quite, like the data loader we used on images. (You'll see shortly that we have to update our training loop to deal with some of the oddities of the Batch interface.)

```
train_iterator, valid_iterator, test_iterator = data.BucketIterator.splits(
(train, valid, test),
batch_size = 32,
device = device)
```

Putting everything together, here's the complete code for building up our datasets:

```
from torchtext import data

device = "cuda"
LABEL = data.LabelField()
TWEET = data.Field(tokenize='spacy', lower=true)

fields = [('score',None), ('id',None),('date',None),('query',None),
        ('name',None),
        ('tweet', TWEET),('category',None),('label',LABEL)]
```

```
twitterDataset = torchtext.data.TabularDataset(
        path="training-processed.csv",
        format="CSV",
        fields=fields,
        skip_header=False)

(train, test, valid) = twitterDataset.split(split_ratio=[0.8,0.1,0.1])

vocab_size = 20002
TWEET.build_vocab(train, max_size = vocab_size)

train_iterator, valid_iterator, test_iterator = data.BucketIterator.splits(
(train, valid, test),
batch_size = 32,
device = device)
```

With our data processing sorted, we can move on to defining our model.

Creating Our Model

We use the `Embedding` and `LSTM` modules in PyTorch that we talked about in the first half of this chapter to build a simple model for classifying tweets:

```
import torch.nn as nn

class OurFirstLSTM(nn.Module):
    def __init__(self, hidden_size, embedding_dim, vocab_size):
        super(OurFirstLSTM, self).__init__()

        self.embedding = nn.Embedding(vocab_size, embedding_dim)
        self.encoder = nn.LSTM(input_size=embedding_dim,
                hidden_size=hidden_size, num_layers=1)
        self.predictor = nn.Linear(hidden_size, 2)

    def forward(self, seq):
        output, (hidden,_) = self.encoder(self.embedding(seq))
        preds = self.predictor(hidden.squeeze(0))
        return preds

model = OurFirstLSTM(100,300, 20002)
model.to(device)
```

All we do in this model is create three layers. First, the words in our tweets are pushed into an `Embedding` layer, which we have established as a 300-dimensional vector embedding. That's then fed into a `LSTM` with 100 hidden features (again, we're compressing down from the 300-dimensional input like we did with images). Finally, the output of the LSTM (the final hidden state after processing the incoming tweet) is pushed through a standard fully connected layer with three outputs to correspond to our three possible classes (negative, positive, or neutral). Next we turn to the training loop!

Updating the Training Loop

Because of some torchtext's quirks, we need to write a slightly modified training loop. First, we create an optimizer (we use Adam as usual) and a loss function. Because we were given three potential classes for each tweet, we use CrossEntropy Loss() as our loss function. However, it turns out that only two classes are present in the dataset; if we assumed there would be only two classes, we could in fact change the output of the model to produce a single number between 0 and 1 and then use binary cross-entropy (BCE) loss (and we can combine the sigmoid layer that squashes output between 0 and 1 plus the BCE layer into a single PyTorch loss function, BCEWithLogitsLoss()). I mention this because if you're writing a classifier that must always be one state or the other, it's a better fit than the standard cross-entropy loss that we're about to use.

```
optimizer = optim.Adam(model.parameters(), lr=2e-2)
criterion = nn.CrossEntropyLoss()

def train(epochs, model, optimizer, criterion, train_iterator, valid_iterator):
    for epoch in range(1, epochs + 1):

        training_loss = 0.0
        valid_loss = 0.0
        model.train()
        for batch_idx, batch in enumerate(train_iterator):
            opt.zero_grad()
            predict = model(batch.tweet)
            loss = criterion(predict,batch.label)
            loss.backward()
            optimizer.step()
            training_loss += loss.data.item() * batch.tweet.size(0)
        training_loss /= len(train_iterator)


        model.eval()
        for batch_idx,batch in enumerate(valid_iterator):
            predict = model(batch.tweet)
            loss = criterion(predict,batch.label)
            valid_loss += loss.data.item() * x.size(0)

        valid_loss /= len(valid_iterator)
        print('Epoch: {}, Training Loss: {:.2f},
        Validation Loss: {:.2f}'.format(epoch, training_loss, valid_loss))
```

The main thing to be aware of in this new training loop is that we have to reference batch.tweet and batch.label to get the particular fields we're interested in; they don't fall out quite as nicely from the enumerator as they do in torchvision.

Once we've trained our model by using this function, we can use it to classify some tweets to do simple sentiment analysis.

Classifying Tweets

Another hassle of `torchtext` is that it's a bit of a pain to get it to predict things. What you can do is emulate the processing pipeline that happens internally and make the required prediction on the output of that pipeline, as shown in this small function:

```
def classify_tweet(tweet):
    categories = {0: "Negative", 1:"Positive"}
    processed = TWEET.process([TWEET.preprocess(tweet)])
    return categories[model(processed).argmax().item()]
```

We have to call `preprocess()`, which performs our spaCy-based tokenization. After that, we can call `process()` to the tokens into a tensor based on our already-built vocabulary. The only thing we have to be careful about is that `torchtext` is expecting a batch of strings, so we have to turn it into a list of lists before handing it off to the processing function. Then we feed it into the model. This will produce a tensor that looks like this:

```
tensor([[ 0.7828, -0.0024]])
```

The tensor element with the highest value corresponds to the model's chosen class, so we use `argmax()` to get the index of that, and then `item()` to turn that zero-dimension tensor into a Python integer that we index into our `categories` dictionary.

With our model trained, let's look at how to do some of the other tricks and techniques that you learned for images in Chapters 2–4.

Data Augmentation

You might wonder exactly how you can augment text data. After all, you can't really flip it horizontally as you can an image! But you can use some techniques with text that will provide the model with a little more information for training. First, you could replace words in the sentence with synonyms, like so:

```
The cat sat on the mat
```

could become

```
The cat sat on the rug
```

Aside from the cat's insistence that a rug is much softer than a mat, the meaning of the sentence hasn't changed. But *mat* and *rug* will be mapped to different indices in the vocabulary, so the model will learn that the two sentences map to the same label, and hopefully that there's a connection between those two words, as everything else in the sentences is the same.

In early 2019, the paper "EDA: Easy Data Augmentation Techniques for Boosting Performance on Text Classification Tasks" suggested three other augmentation strategies: random insertion, random swap, and random deletion. Let's take a look at each of them.[3]

Random Insertion

A *random insertion* technique looks at a sentence and then randomly inserts synonyms of existing nonstop-words into the sentence *n* times. Assuming you have a way of getting a synonym of a word and a way of eliminating stop-words (common words such as *and, it, the*, etc.), shown, but not implemented, in this function via `get_syno nyms()` and `get_stopwords()`, an implementation of this would be as follows:

```
def random_insertion(sentence,n):
    words = remove_stopwords(sentence)
    for _ in range(n):
        new_synonym = get_synonyms(random.choice(words))
        sentence.insert(randrange(len(sentence)+1), new_synonym)
    return sentence
```

An example of this in practice where it replaces cat could look like this:

```
The cat sat on the mat
The cat mat sat on feline the mat
```

Random Deletion

As the name suggests, *random deletion* deletes words from a sentence. Given a probability parameter p, it will go through the sentence and decide whether to delete a word or not based on that random probability:

```
def random_deletion(words, p=0.5):
    if len(words) == 1:
        return words
    remaining = list(filter(lambda x: random.uniform(0,1) > p,words))
    if len(remaining) == 0:
        return [random.choice(words)]
    else
        return remaining
```

The implementation deals with the edge cases—if there's only one word, the technique returns it; and if we end up deleting all the words in the sentence, the technique samples a random word from the original set.

---

3 See "EDA: Easy Data Augmentation Techniques for Boosting Performance on Text Classification Tasks" (*https://arxiv.org/abs/1901.11196*) by Jason W. Wei and Kai Zou (2019).

Random Swap

The *random swap* augmentation takes a sentence and then swaps words within it n times, with each iteration working on the previously swapped sentence. Here's an implementation:

```python
def random_swap(sentence, n=5):
    length = range(len(sentence))
    for _ in range(n):
        idx1, idx2 = random.sample(length, 2)
        sentence[idx1], sentence[idx2] = sentence[idx2], sentence[idx1]
    return sentence
```

We sample two random numbers based on the length of the sentence, and then just keep swapping until we hit n.

The techniques in the EDA paper average about a 3% improvement in accuracy when used with small amounts of labeled examples (roughly 500). If you have more than 5,000 examples in your dataset, the paper suggests that this improvement may fall to 0.8% or lower, due to the model obtaining better generalization from the larger amounts of data available over the improvements that EDA can provide.

Back Translation

Another popular approach for augmenting datasets is *back translation*. This involves translating a sentence from our target language into one or more other languages and then translating all of them back to the original language. We can use the Python library `googletrans` for this purpose. Install it with `pip`, as it doesn't appear to be in conda at the time of this writing:

```
pip install googletrans
```

Then, we can translate our sentence from English to French, and then back to English:

```python
import googletrans
import googletrans.Translator

translator = Translator()

sentences = ['The cat sat on the mat']

translation_fr = translator.translate(sentences, dest='fr')
fr_text = [t.text for t in translations_fr]
translation_en = translator.translate(fr_text, dest='en')
en_text = [t.text for t in translation_en]
print(en_text)

>> ['The cat sat on the carpet']
```

That gives us an augmented sentence from English to French and back again, but let's go a step further and select a language at random:

```
import random

available_langs = list(googletrans.LANGUAGES.keys())
tr_lang = random.choice(available_langs)
print(f"Translating to {googletrans.LANGUAGES[tr_lang]}")

translations = translator.translate(sentences, dest=tr_lang)
t_text = [t.text for t in translations]
print(t_text)

translations_en_random = translator.translate(t_text, src=tr_lang, dest='en')
en_text = [t.text for t in translations_en_random]
print(en_text)
```

In this case, we use `random.choice` to grab a random language, translate to that language, and then translate back as before. We also pass in the language to the `src` parameter just to help the language detection of Google Translate along. Try it out and see how much it resembles the old game of *Telephone*.

You need to be aware of a few limits. First, you can translate only up to 15,000 characters at a time, though that shouldn't be too much of a problem if you're just translating sentences. Second, if you are going to use this on a large dataset, you want to do your data augmentation on a cloud instance rather than your home computer, because if Google bans your IP, you won't be able to use Google Translate for normal use! Make sure that you send a few batches at a time rather than the entire dataset at once. This should also allow you to restart translation batches if there's an error on the Google Translate backend as well.

Augmentation and torchtext

You might have noticed that everything I've said so far about augmentation hasn't involved `torchtext`. Sadly, there's a reason for that. Unlike `torchvision` or `torchaudio`, `torchtext` doesn't offer a transform pipeline, which is a little annoying. It does offer a way of performing pre- and post-processing, but this operates only on the token (word) level, which is perhaps enough for synonym replacement, but doesn't provide enough control for something like back translation. And if you do try to hijack the pipelines for augmentation, you should probably do it in the preprocessing pipeline instead of the post-processing one, as all you'll see in that one is the tensor that consists of integers, which you'll have to map to words via the vocab rules.

For these reasons, I suggest not even bothering with spending your time trying to twist `torchtext` into knots to do data augmentation. Instead, do the augmentation outside PyTorch using techniques such as back translation to generate new data and feed that into the model as if it were *real* data.

That's augmentation covered, but there's an elephant in the room that we should address before wrapping up the chapter.

Transfer Learning?

You might be wondering why we haven't talked about transfer learning yet. After all, it's a key technique that allows us to create accurate image-based models, so why can't we do that here? Well, it turns out that it has been a little harder to get transfer learning working on LSTM networks. But not impossible. We'll return to the subject in Chapter 9, where you'll see how to get transfer learning working with both the LSTM- and Transformer-based networks.

Conclusion

In this chapter, we covered a text-processing pipeline that covers encoding and embeddings, a simple LSTM-based neural network to perform classification, along with some data augmentation strategies for text-based data. You have plenty to experiment with so far. I've chosen to make every tweet lowercase during the tokenization phase. This is a popular approach in NLP, but it does throw away potential information in the tweet. Think about it: "Why is this NOT WORKING?" to our eyes is even more suggestive of a negative sentiment than "Why is this not working?" but we've thrown away that difference between the two tweets before it even hits the model. So definitely try running with case sensitivity left in the tokenized text. And try removing stop-words from your input text to see whether that helps improve the accuracy. Traditional NLP methods make a big point of removing them, but I've often found that deep learning techniques can perform better when leaving them in the input (which we've done in this chapter). This is because they provide more context for the model to learn from, whereas sentences that have been reduced to *only* important words may be missing nuances in the text.

You may also want to alter the size of the embedding vector. Larger vectors mean that the embedding can capture more information about the word it's modeling at the cost of using more memory. Try going from 100- to 1,000-dimensional embeddings and see how that affects training time and accuracy.

Finally, you can also play with the LSTM. We've used a simple approach, but you can increase `num_layers` to create stacked LSTMs, increase or decrease the number of hidden features in the layer, or set `bidirectional=true` to create a biLSTM. Replacing the entire LSTM with a GRU layer would also be an interesting thing to try; does it train faster? Is it more accurate? Experiment and see what you find!

In the meantime, we move on from text and into the audio realm with `torchaudio`.

Further Reading

- "Long Short-term Memory" (*https://oreil.ly/WKcxO*) by S. Hochreiter and J. Schmidhuber (1997)
- "Learning Phrase Representations Using RNN Encoder-Decoder for Statistical Machine Translation" (*https://arxiv.org/abs/1406.1078*) by Kyunghyun Cho et al. (2014)
- "Bidirectional LSTM-CRF Models for Sequence Tagging" (*https://arxiv.org/abs/1508.01991*) by Zhiheng Huang et al. (2015)
- "Attention Is All You Need" (*https://arxiv.org/abs/1706.03762*) by Ashish Vaswani et al. (2017)

CHAPTER 6

A Journey into Sound

One of the most successful applications of deep learning is something that we carry around with us every day. Whether it's Siri or Google Now, the engines that power both systems and Amazon's Alexa are neural networks. In this chapter, we'll take a look at PyTorch's torchaudio library. You'll learn how to use it to construct a pipeline for classifying audio data with a convolutional based model. After that, I'll suggest a different approach that will allow you to use some of the tricks you learned for images and obtain good accuracy on the ESC-50 audio dataset.

But first, let's take a look at sound itself. What is it? How is it often represented in data form, and does that provide us with any clues as to what type of neural net we should use to gain insight from our data?

Sound

Sound is created via the vibration of air. All the sounds we hear are combinations of high and low pressure that we often represent in a waveform, like the one in Figure 6-1. In this image, the wave above the origin is high pressure, and the part below is low pressure.

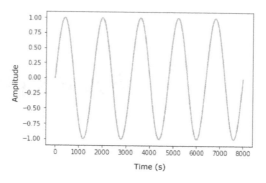

Figure 6-1. Sine wave

Figure 6-2 shows a more complex waveform of a complete song.

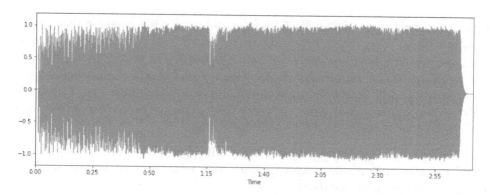

Figure 6-2. Song waveform

In digital sound, we *sample* this waveform many times a second, traditionally 44,100 for CD-quality sound, and store the amplitude values of the wave during each sample point. At a time t, we have a single value stored. This is slightly different from an image, which requires two values, x and y, to store a value (for a grayscale image). If we use convolutional filters in our neural network, we need a 1D filter rather than the 2D filters we were using for images.

Now that you know a little more about sound, let's look at the dataset we use so you can get a little more familiar with it.

The ESC-50 Dataset

The *Environmental Sound Classification* (ESC) dataset is a collection of field recordings, each of which is 5 seconds long and assigned to one of 50 classes (e.g., a dog barking, snoring, a knock on a door). We use this set for the rest of the chapter to experiment with two ways of classifying audio, as well as to explore using `torchaudio` to simplify loading and manipulating audio.

Obtaining the Dataset

The ESC-50 dataset (*https://github.com/karoldvl/ESC-50*) is a set of WAV files. You can download it either by cloning the Git repository:

    git clone https://github.com/karoldvl/ESC-50

Or you can download the entire repo just by using curl:

    curl https://github.com/karoldvl/ESC-50/archive/master.zip

All the WAV files are stored in the *audio* directory with filenames like this:

    1-100032-A-0.wav

We care about the final number in the filename, because that tells us what class this sound clip has been assigned to. The other parts of the filename don't matter to us but mostly relate to the larger Freesound dataset from which ESC-50 has been drawn (with one exception that I'll come back to shortly). If you're interested in finding out more, the *README* document in the ESC-50 repo goes into further detail.

Now that we've downloaded the dataset, let's look at some of the sounds it contains.

Playing Audio in Jupyter

If you want to actually hear a sound from ESC-50, then instead of loading one of the files into a standard music player such as iTunes, you can use Jupyter's built-in player for audio, `IPython.display.Audio`:

```
import IPython.display as display
display.Audio('ESC-50/audio/1-100032-A-0.wav')
```

The function will read in our WAV files and MP3 files. You can also generate tensors, convert them into NumPy arrays, and play those directly. Play some of the files in the *ESC-50* directory to get a feel for the sounds available. Once you've done that, we'll explore the dataset in depth a little more.

Exploring ESC-50

When dealing with a new dataset, it's always a good idea to get a feeling for the *shape* of the data before you dive right into building models. In classification tasks, for example, you'll want to know whether your dataset actually contains examples from all the possible classes, and ideally that all classes are present in equal numbers. Let's take a look at how ESC-50 breaks down.

 If your dataset has an *unbalanced* amount of data, a simple solution is to randomly duplicate the smaller class examples until you have increased them to the number of the other classes. Although this feels like fake accounting, it's surprisingly effective (and cheap!) in practice.

We know that the final set of digits in each filename describes the class it belongs to, so what we need to do is grab a list of the files and count up the occurrences of each class:

```
import glob
from collections import Counter

esc50_list = [f.split("-")[-1].replace(".wav","")
        for f in
        glob.glob("ESC-50/audio/*.wav")]
Counter(esc50_list)
```

First, we build up a list of our ESC-50 filenames. Because we care about only the class number at the end of the filename, we chop off the *.wav* extension and split the filename on the - separator. We finally take the last element in that split string. If you inspect esc50_list, you'll get a bunch of strings that range from 0 to 49. We could write more code that builds a dict and counts all the occurrences for us, but I'm lazy, so I'm using a Python convenience function, Counter, that does all that for us.

Here's the output!

```
Counter({'15': 40,
    '22': 40,
    '36': 40,
    '44': 40,
    '23': 40,
    '31': 40,
    '9': 40,
    '13': 40,
    '4': 40,
    '3': 40,
    '27': 40,
    ...})
```

We have one of those rare things, a perfectly balanced dataset. Let's break out the champagne and install a few more libraries that we're going to need shortly.

SoX and LibROSA

Most of the audio processing that `torchaudio` carries out relies on two other pieces of software: *SoX* and *LibROSA*. *LibROSA* (*https://github.com/librosa/librosa*) is a Python library for audio analysis, including generating mel spectrograms (You'll see what these are a little later in the chapter), detecting beats, and even generating music.

SoX, on the other hand, is a program that you might already be familiar with if you've been using Linux for years. In fact, *SoX* is so old that it predates Linux itself; its first release was in July 1991, compared to the Linux debut in September 1991. I remember using it back in 1997 to convert WAV files into MP3s on my first ever Linux box. But it's still useful![1]

If you're installing `torchaudio` via `conda`, you can skip to the next section. If you're using `pip`, you'll probably need to install *SoX* itself. For a Red Hat-based system, enter the following:

```
yum install sox
```

Or on a Debian-based system, you'll use this:

```
apt intall sox
```

Once *SoX* is installed, you can move on to obtaining `torchaudio` itself.

torchaudio

Installing `torchaudio` can be performed with either `conda` or `pip`:

```
conda install -c derickl torchaudio
pip install torchaudio
```

In comparison with `torchvision`, `torchaudio` is similar to `torchtext` in that it's not quite as well loved, maintained, or documented. I'd expect this to change in the near future as PyTorch gets more popular and better text and audio handling pipelines are created. Still, `torchaudio` is plenty for our needs; we just have to write some custom dataloaders (which we didn't have to do for audio or text processing).

Anyhow, the core of `torchaudio` is found within `load()` and `save()`. We're concerned only with `load()` in this chapter, but you'll need to use `save()` if you're generating new audio from your input (e.g., a text-to-speech model). `load()` takes a file

---

1 Understanding all of what *SoX* can do (*http://sox.sourceforge.net*) is beyond the scope of this book, and won't be necessary for what we're going to be doing in the rest of this chapter.

specified in `filepath` and returns a tensor representation of the audio file and the sample rate of that audio file as a separate variable.

We now have the means for loading one of the WAV files from the ESC-50 dataset and turning it into a tensor. Unlike our earlier work with text and images, we need to write a bit more code before we can get on with creating and training a model. We need to write a custom *dataset*.

Building an ESC-50 Dataset

We've talked about datasets in Chapter 2, but `torchvision` and `torchtext` did all the heavy lifting for us, so we didn't have to worry too much about the details. As you may remember, a custom dataset has to implement two class methods, __getitem__ and __len__, so that the data loader can get a batch of tensors and their labels, as well as a total count of tensors in the dataset. We also have an __init__ method for setting up things like file paths that'll be used over and over again.

Here's our first pass at the ESC-50 dataset:

```
class ESC50(Dataset):

    def __init__(self,path):
        # Get directory listing from path
        files = Path(path).glob('*.wav')
        # Iterate through the listing and create a list of tuples (filename, label)
        self.items = [(f,int(f.name.split("-")[-1]
                    .replace(".wav",""))) for f in files]
        self.length = len(self.items)

    def __getitem__(self, index):
        filename, label = self.items[index]
        audio_tensor, sample_rate = torchaudio.load(filename)
        return audio_tensor, label

    def __len__(self):
        return self.length
```

The majority of the work in the class happens when a new instance of it is created. The __init__ method takes the `path` parameter, finds all the WAV files inside that path, and then produces tuples of *(filename, label)* by using the same string split we used earlier in the chapter to get the label of that audio sample. When PyTorch requests an item from the dataset, we index into the `items` list, use `torchaudio.load` to make `torchaudio` load in the audio file, turn it into a tensor, and then return both the tensor and the label.

And that's enough for us to start with. For a sanity check, let's create an `ESC50` object and extract the first item:

```
test_esc50 = ESC50(PATH_TO_ESC50)
tensor, label = list(test_esc50)[0]

tensor
```

```
tensor([-0.0128, -0.0131, -0.0143,  ...,  0.0000,  0.0000,  0.0000])

tensor.shape
torch.Size([220500])

label
'15'
```

We can construct a data loader by using standard PyTorch constructs:

```
example_loader = torch.utils.data.DataLoader(test_esc50, batch_size = 64,
shuffle = True)
```

But before we do that, we have to go back to our data. As you might remember, we should always create training, validation, and test sets. At the moment, we have just one directory with all the data, which is no good for our purposes. A 60/20/20 split of data into training, validation, and test collections should suffice. Now, we could do this by taking random samples of our entire dataset (taking care to sample without replacement and making sure that our newly constructed datasets are still balanced), but again the ESC-50 dataset saves us from having to do much work. The compilers of the dataset separated the data into five equal balanced *folds*, indicated by the *first* digit in the filename. We'll have folds 1,2,3 be the training set, 4 the validation set, and 5 the test set. But feel free to mix it up if you don't want to be boring and consecutive! Move each of the folds to *test*, *train*, and *validation* directories:

```
mv 1* ../train
mv 2* ../train
mv 3* ../train
mv 4* ../valid
mv 5* ../test
```

Now we can create the individual datasets and loaders:

```
from pathlib import Path

bs=64
PATH_TO_ESC50 = Path.cwd() / 'esc50'
path =  'test.md'
test

train_esc50 = ESC50(PATH_TO_ESC50 / "train")
valid_esc50 = ESC50(PATH_TO_ESC50 / "valid")
test_esc50  = ESC50(PATH_TO_ESC50 / "test")

train_loader = torch.utils.data.DataLoader(train_esc50, batch_size = bs,
                shuffle = True)
valid_loader = torch.utils.data.DataLoader(valid_esc50, batch_size = bs,
                shuffle = True)
test_loader  = torch.utils.data.DataLoader(test_esc50, batch_size = bs,
                shuffle = True)
```

We have our data all set up, so we're all ready to look at a classification model.

A CNN Model for ESC-50

For our first attempt at classifying sounds, we build a model that borrows heavily from a paper called "Very Deep Convolutional Networks For Raw Waveforms."[2] You'll see that it uses a lot of our building blocks from Chapter 3, but instead of using 2D layers, we're using 1D variants, as we have one fewer dimension in our audio input:

```python
class AudioNet(nn.Module):
    def __init__(self):
        super(AudioNet, self).__init__()
        self.conv1 = nn.Conv1d(1, 128, 80, 4)
        self.bn1 = nn.BatchNorm1d(128)
        self.pool1 = nn.MaxPool1d(4)
        self.conv2 = nn.Conv1d(128, 128, 3)
        self.bn2 = nn.BatchNorm1d(128)
        self.pool2 = nn.MaxPool1d(4)
        self.conv3 = nn.Conv1d(128, 256, 3)
        self.bn3 = nn.BatchNorm1d(256)
        self.pool3 = nn.MaxPool1d(4)
        self.conv4 = nn.Conv1d(256, 512, 3)
        self.bn4 = nn.BatchNorm1d(512)
        self.pool4 = nn.MaxPool1d(4)
        self.avgPool = nn.AvgPool1d(30)
        self.fc1 = nn.Linear(512, 10)

    def forward(self, x):
        x = self.conv1(x)
        x = F.relu(self.bn1(x))
        x = self.pool1(x)
        x = self.conv2(x)
        x = F.relu(self.bn2(x))
        x = self.pool2(x)
        x = self.conv3(x)
        x = F.relu(self.bn3(x))
        x = self.pool3(x)
        x = self.conv4(x)
        x = F.relu(self.bn4(x))
        x = self.pool4(x)
        x = self.avgPool(x)
        x = x.permute(0, 2, 1)
        x = self.fc1(x)
        return F.log_softmax(x, dim = 2)
```

---

2 See "Very Deep Convolutional Neural Networks for Raw Waveforms" (*https://arxiv.org/pdf/1610.00087.pdf*) by Wei Dai et al. (2016).

We also need an optimizer and a loss function. For the optimizer, we use Adam as before, but what loss function do you think we should use? (If you answered `CrossEn tropyLoss`, give yourself a gold star!)

```
audio_net = AudioNet()
audio_net.to(device)
```

Having created our model, we save our weights and use the `find_lr()` function from Chapter 4:

```
audio_net.save("audionet.pth")
import torch.optim as optim
optimizer = optim.Adam(audionet.parameters(), lr=0.001)
logs,losses = find_lr(audio_net, nn.CrossEntropyLoss(), optimizer)
plt.plot(logs,losses)
```

From the plot in Figure 6-3, we determine that the appropriate learning rate is around `1e-5` (based on where the descent looks steepest). We set that to be our learning rate and reload our model's initial weights:

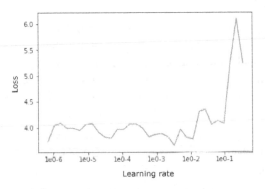

Figure 6-3. AudioNet learning rate plot

```
lr = 1e-5
model.load("audionet.pth")
import torch.optim as optim
optimizer = optim.Adam(audionet.parameters(), lr=lr)
```

We train the model for 20 epochs:

```
train(audio_net, optimizer, torch.nn.CrossEntropyLoss(),
train_data_loader, valid_data_loader, epochs=20)
```

After training, you should find that the model attains around 13%–17% accuracy on our dataset. That's better than the 2% we could expect if we were just picking one of the 50 classes at random. But perhaps we can do better; let's investigate a different way of looking at our audio data that may yield better results.

This Frequency Is My Universe

If you look back at the GitHub page for ESC-50, you'll see a leaderboard of network architectures and their accuracy scores. You'll notice that in comparison, we're not doing great. We could extend the model we've created to be deeper, and that would likely increase our accuracy a little, but for a real increase in performance, we need to switch domains. In audio processing, you can work on the pure waveform as we've been doing; but most of the time, you'll work in the *frequency domain*. This different representation transforms the raw waveform into a view that shows all of the frequencies of sound at a given point in time. This is perhaps a more information-rich representation to present to a neural network, as it'll be able to work on those frequencies directly, rather than having to work out how to map the raw waveform signal into something the model can use.

Let's look at how to generate frequency spectrograms with *LibROSA*.

Mel Spectrograms

Traditionally, getting into the frequency domain requires applying the Fourier transform on the audio signal. We're going to go beyond that a little by generating our spectrograms in the mel scale. The *mel scale* defines a scale of pitches that are equal in distance from another, where 1000 mels = 1000 Hz. This scale is commonly used in audio processing, especially in speech recognition and classification applications. Producing a mel spectrogram with *LibROSA* requires two lines of code:

```
sample_data, sr = librosa.load("ESC-50/train/1-100032-A-0.wav", sr=None)
spectrogram = librosa.feature.melspectrogram(sample_data, sr=sr)
```

This results in a NumPy array containing the spectrogram data. If we display this spectrogram as shown in Figure 6-4, we can see the frequencies in our sound:

```
librosa.display.specshow(spectrogram, sr=sr, x_axis='time', y_axis='mel')
```

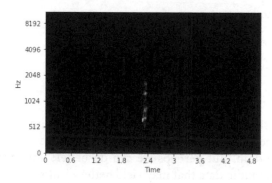

Figure 6-4. Mel spectrogram

However, not a lot of information is present in the image. We can do better! If we convert the spectrogram to a logarithmic scale, we can see a lot more of the audio's structure, due to the scale being able to represent a wider range of values. And this is common enough in audio procressing that *LibROSA* includes a method for it:

```
log_spectrogram = librosa.power_to_db(spectrogram, ref=np.max)
```

This computes a scaling factor of `10 * log10(spectrogram / ref)`. `ref` defaults to `1.0`, but here we're passing in `np.max()` so that `spectrogram / ref` will fall within the range of `[0,1]`. Figure 6-5 shows the new spectrogram.

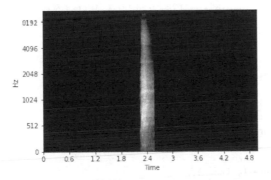

Figure 6-5. Log mel spectrogram

We now have a log-scaled mel spectrogram! If you call `log_spectrogram.shape`, you'll see it's a 2D tensor, which makes sense because we've plotted images with the tensor. We could create a new neural network architecture and feed this new data into it, but I have a diabolical trick up my sleeve. We literally just generated images of the spectrogram data. Why don't we work on those instead?

This might seem silly at first; after all, we have the underlying spectrogram data, and that's more exact than the image representation (to our eyes, knowing that a data point is 58 rather than 60 means *more* to us than a different shade of, say, purple). And if we were starting from scratch, that'd definitely be the case. But! We have, just lying around the place, already-trained networks such as ResNet and Inception that we *know* are amazing at recognizing structure and other parts of images. We can construct image representations of our audio and use a pretrained network to make big jumps in accuracy with very little training by using the super power of transfer learning once again. This could be useful with our dataset, as we don't have a lot of examples (only 2,000!) to train our network.

This trick can be employed across many disparate datasets. If you can find a way of cheaply turning your data into an image representation, it's worth doing that and throwing a ResNet network against it to get a baseline of what transfer learning can do for you, so you know what you have to beat by using a different approach. Armed with this, let's create a new dataset that will generate these images for us on demand.

A New Dataset

Now throw away the original ESC50 dataset class and build a new one, ESC50Spectro gram. Although this will share some code with the older class, quite a lot more is going on in the __get_item__ method in this version. We generate the spectrogram by using *LibROSA*, and then we do some fancy matplotlib footwork to get the data into a NumPy array. We apply the array to our transformation pipeline (which just uses ToTensor) and return that and the item's label. Here's the code:

```
class ESC50Spectrogram(Dataset):

    def __init__(self,path):
        files = Path(path).glob('*.wav')
        self.items = [(f,int(f.name.split("-")[-1].replace(".wav","")))
                        for f in files]
        self.length = len(self.items)
        self.transforms = torchvision.transforms.Compose(
                    [torchvision.transforms.ToTensor()])

    def __getitem__(self, index):
        filename, label = self.items[index]
        audio_tensor, sample_rate = librosa.load(filename, sr=None)
        spectrogram = librosa.feature.melspectrogram(audio_tensor, sr=sample_rate)
        log_spectrogram = librosa.power_to_db(spectrogram, ref=np.max)
        librosa.display.specshow(log_spectrogram, sr=sample_rate,
                            x_axis='time', y_axis='mel')
        plt.gcf().canvas.draw()
        audio_data = np.frombuffer(fig.canvas.tostring_rgb(), dtype=np.uint8)
        audio_data = audio_data.reshape(fig.canvas.get_width_height()[::-1] + (3,))
        return (self.transforms(audio_data), label)

    def __len__(self):
        return self.length
```

We're not going to spend too much time on this version of the dataset because it has a large flaw, which I demonstrate with Python's process_time() method:

```
oldESC50 = ESC50("ESC-50/train/")
start_time = time.process_time()
oldESC50.__getitem__(33)
end_time = time.process_time()
old_time = end_time - start_time

newESC50 = ESC50Spectrogram("ESC-50/train/")
start_time = time.process_time()
newESC50.__getitem__(33)
end_time = time.process_time()
new_time = end_time - start_time
```

```
old_time = 0.004786839000075815
new_time = 0.39544327499993415
```

The new dataset is almost one hundred times slower than our original one that just returned the raw audio! That will make training incredibly slow, and may even negate any of the benefits we could get from using transfer learning.

We can use a couple of tricks to get around most of our troubles here. The first approach would be to add a cache to store the generated spectrogram in memory, so we don't have to regenerate it every time the __getitem__ method is called. Using Python's functools package, we can do this easily:

```
import functools

class ESC50Spectrogram(Dataset):
 #skipping init code

    @functools.lru_cache(maxsize=<size of dataset>)
    def __getitem__(self, index):
```

Provided you have enough memory to store the entire contents of the dataset into RAM, this may be good enough. We've set up a *least recently used* (LRU) cache that will keep the contents in memory for as long as possible, with indices that haven't been accessed recently being the first for ejection from the cache when memory gets tight. However, if you don't have enough memory to store everything, you'll hit slow-downs on every batch iteration as ejected spectrograms need to be regenerated.

My preferred approach is to *precompute* all the possible plots and then create a new custom dataset class that loads these images from the disk. (You can even add the LRU cache annotation as well for further speed-up.)

We don't need to do anything fancy for precomputing, just a method that saves the plots into the same directory it's traversing:

```
def precompute_spectrograms(path, dpi=50):
    files = Path(path).glob('*.wav')
    for filename in files:
        audio_tensor, sample_rate = librosa.load(filename, sr=None)
        spectrogram = librosa.feature.melspectrogram(audio_tensor, sr=sr)
        log_spectrogram = librosa.power_to_db(spectrogram, ref=np.max)
        librosa.display.specshow(log_spectrogram, sr=sr, x_axis='time',
                                 y_axis='mel')
        plt.gcf().savefig("{}{}_{}.png".format(filename.parent,dpi,
                            filename.name),dpi=dpi)
```

This method is simpler than our previous dataset because we can use matplotlib's savefig method to save a plot directly to disk rather than having to mess around with NumPy. We also provide an additional input parameter, dpi, which allows us to control the quality of the generated output. Run this on all the train, test, and valid paths that we have already set up (it will likely take a couple of hours to get through all the images).

All we need now is a new dataset that reads these images. We can't use the standard `ImageDataLoader` from Chapters 2–4, as the PNG filename scheme doesn't match the directory structure that it uses. But no matter, we can just open an image by using the Python Imaging Library:

```
from PIL import Image

class PrecomputedESC50(Dataset):
    def __init__(self,path,dpi=50, transforms=None):
        files = Path(path).glob('{}*.wav.png'.format(dpi))
        self.items = [(f,int(f.name.split("-")[-1]
        .replace(".wav.png",""))) for f in files]
        self.length = len(self.items)
        if transforms=None:
            self.transforms =
            torchvision.transforms.Compose([torchvision.transforms.ToTensor()])
        else:
            self.transforms = transforms

    def __getitem__(self, index):
        filename, label = self.items[index]
        img = Image.open(filename)
        return (self.transforms(img), label)

    def __len__(self):
        return self.length
```

This code is much simpler, and hopefully that's also reflected in the time it takes to get an entry from the dataset:

```
start_time = time.process_time()
b.__getitem__(33)
end_time = time.process_time()
end_time - start_time
>> 0.0031465259999094997
```

Obtaining an element from this dataset takes roughly the same time as in our original audio-based one, so we won't be losing anything by moving to our image-based approach, except for the one-time cost of precomputing all the images before creating the database. We've also supplied a default transform pipeline that turns an image into a tensor, but it can be swapped out for a different pipeline during initialization. Armed with these optimizations, we can start to apply transfer learning to the problem.

A Wild ResNet Appears

As you may remember from Chapter 4, transfer learning requires that we take a model that has already been trained on a particular dataset (in the case of images, likely ImageNet), and then fine-tune it on our particular data domain, the ESC-50 dataset that we're turning into spectrogram images. You might be wondering whether a model that is trained on *normal* photographs is of any use to us. It turns out that the pretrained models *do* learn a lot of structure that can be applied to domains that at first glance might seem wildly different. Here's our code from Chapter 4 that initializes a model:

```
from torchvision import models
spec_resnet = models.ResNet50(pretrained=True)

for param in spec_resnet.parameters():
    param.requires_grad = False

spec_resnet.fc = nn.Sequential(nn.Linear(spec_resnet.fc.in_features,500),
nn.ReLU(),
nn.Dropout(), nn.Linear(500,50))
```

This initializes us with a pretrained (and frozen) `ResNet50` model and swaps out the head of the model for an untrained `Sequential` module that ends with a `Linear` with an output of 50, one for each of the classes in the ESC-50 dataset. We also need to create a `DataLoader` that takes our precomputed spectrograms. When we create our ESC-50 dataset, we'll also want to normalize the incoming images with the standard ImageNet standard deviation and mean, as that's what the pretrained ResNet-50 architecture was trained with. We can do that by passing in a new pipeline:

```
esc50pre_train = PreparedESC50(PATH, transforms=torchvision.transforms
.Compose([torchvision.transforms.ToTensor(),
torchvision.transforms.Normalize
(mean=[0.485, 0.456, 0.406],
std=[0.229, 0.224, 0.225])]))

esc50pre_valid = PreparedESC50(PATH, transforms=torchvision.transforms
.Compose([torchvision.transforms.ToTensor(),
torchvision.transforms.Normalize
(mean=[0.485, 0.456, 0.406],
std=[0.229, 0.224, 0.225])]))


esc50_train_loader = (esc50pre_train, bs, shuffle=True)
esc50_valid_loader = (esc50pre_valid, bs, shuffle=True)
```

With our data loaders set up, we can move on to finding a learning rate and get ready to train.

Finding a Learning Rate

We need to find a learning rate to use in our model. As in Chapter 4, we'll save the model's initial parameters and use our `find_lr()` function to find a decent learning rate for training. Figure 6-6 shows the plot of the losses against the learning rate.

```
spec_resnet.save("spec_resnet.pth")
loss_fn = nn.CrossEntropyLoss()
```

```
optimizer = optim.Adam(spec_resnet.parameters(), lr=lr)
logs,losses = find_lr(spec_resnet, loss_fn, optimizer)
plt.plot(logs, losses)
```

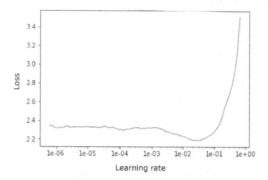

Figure 6-6. A SpecResNet learning rate plot

Looking at the graph of the learning rate plotted against loss, it seems like `1e-2` is a good place to start. As our ResNet-50 model is somewhat deeper than our previous one, we're also going to use differential learning rates of [`1e-2,1e-4,1e-8`], with the highest learning rate applied to our classifier (as it requires the most training!) and slower rates for the already-trained backbone. Again, we use Adam as our optimizer, but feel free to experiment with the others available.

Before we apply those differential rates, though, we train for a few epochs that update only the classifier, as we *froze* the ResNet-50 backbone when we created our network:

```
optimizer = optim.Adam(spec_resnet.parameters(), lr=[1e-2,1e-4,1e-8])

train(spec_resnet, optimizer, nn.CrossEntropyLoss(),
esc50_train_loader, esc50_val_loader,epochs=5,device="cuda")
```

We now unfreeze the backbone and apply our differential rates:

```
for param in spec_resnet.parameters():
    param.requires_grad = True

optimizer = optim.Adam(spec_resnet.parameters(), lr=[1e-2,1e-4,1e-8])

train(spec_resnet, optimizer, nn.CrossEntropyLoss(),
esc50_train_loader, esc50_val_loader,epochs=20,device="cuda")

> Epoch 19, accuracy = 0.80
```

As you can see, with a validation accuracy of around 80%, we're already vastly outperforming our original `AudioNet` model. The power of transfer learning strikes again! Feel free to train for more epochs to see if your accuracy continues to improve. If we look at the ESC-50 leaderboard, we're closing in on human-level accuracy. And that's just with ResNet-50. You could try with ResNet-101 and perhaps an ensemble of different architectures to push the score up even higher.

And there's data augmentation to consider. Let's take a look at a few ways of doing that in both domains that we've been working in so far.

Audio Data Augmentation

When we were looking at images in Chapter 4, we saw that we could improve the accuracy of our classifier by making changes to our incoming pictures. By flipping them, cropping them, or applying other transformations, we made our neural network work harder in the training phase and obtained a more *generalized* model at the end of it, one that was not simply fitting to the data presented (the scourge of overfitting, don't forget). Can we do the same here? Yes! In fact, there are two approaches that we can use—one obvious approach that works on the original audio waveform, and a perhaps less-obvious idea that arises from our decision to use a ResNet-based classifier on images of mel spectrograms. Let's take a look at audio transforms first.

torchaudio Transforms

In a similar manner to `torchvision`, `torchaudio` includes a `transforms` module that perform transformations on incoming data. However, the number of transformations offered is somewhat sparse, especially compared to the plethora that we get when we're working with images. If you're interested, have a look at the documentation (*https://oreil.ly/d1kp6*) for a full list, but the only one we look at here is `torchaudio.transforms.PadTrim`. In the ESC-50 dataset, we are fortunate in that every audio clip is the same length. That isn't something that happens in the real world, but our neural networks like (and sometimes insist on, depending on how they're constructed) input data to be regular. `PadTrim` will take an incoming audio tensor and either pad it out to the required length, or trim it down so it doesn't exceed that length. If we wanted to trim down a clip to a new length, we'd use `PadTrim` like this:

```
audio_tensor, rate = torchaudio.load("test.wav")
audio_tensor.shape
trimmed_tensor = torchaudio.transforms.PadTrim(max_len=1000)(audio_orig)
```

However, if you're looking for augmentation that actually changes how the audio sounds (e.g., adding an echo, noise, or changing the tempo of the clip), then the `torchaudio.transforms` module is of no use to you. Instead, we need to use *SoX*.

SoX Effect Chains

Why it's not part of the `transforms` module, I'm really not sure, but `torchaudio.sox_effects.SoxEffectsChain` allows you to create a chain of one or more *SoX* effects and apply those to an input file. The interface is a bit fiddly, so let's see it in action in a new version of the dataset that changes the pitch of the audio file:

```
class ESC50WithPitchChange(Dataset):

    def __init__(self,path):
        # Get directory listing from path
        files = Path(path).glob('*.wav')
        # Iterate through the listing and create a list of tuples (filename, label)
        self.items = [(f,f.name.split("-")[-1].replace(".wav","")) for f in files]
        self.length = len(self.items)
        self.E = torchaudio.sox_effects.SoxEffectsChain()
        self.E.append_effect_to_chain("pitch", [0.5])

    def __getitem__(self, index):
        filename, label = self.items[index]
        self.E.set_input_file(filename)
        audio_tensor, sample_rate = self.E.sox_build_flow_effects()
        return audio_tensor, label

    def __len__(self):
        return self.length
```

In our __init__ method, we create a new instance variable, E, a SoxEffectsChain, that will contain all the effects that we want to apply to our audio data. We then add a new effect by using append_effect_to_chain, which takes a string indicating the name of the effect, and an array of parameters to send to sox. You can get a list of available effects by calling torchaudio.sox_effects.effect_names(). If we were to add another effect, it would take place after the pitch effect we have already set up, so if you want to create a list of separate effects and randomly apply them, you'll need to create separate chains for each one.

When it comes to selecting an item to return to the data loader, things are a little different. Instead of using torchaudio.load(), we refer to our effects chain and point it to the file by using set_input_file. But note that this doesn't load the file! Instead, we have to use sox_build_flow_effects(), which kicks off *SoX* in the background, applies the effects in the chain, and returns the tensor and sample rate information we would have otherwise obtained from load().

The number of things that *SoX* can do is pretty staggering, and I won't go into more detail on all the possible effects you could use. I suggest having a look at the *SoX* documentation (*https://oreil.ly/uLBTF*) in conjunction with list_effects() to see the possibilities.

These transformations allow us to alter the original audio, but we've spent quite a bit of this chapter building up a processing pipeline that works on images of mel spectrograms. We could do what we did to generate the initial dataset for that pipeline, by creating altered audio samples and then creating the spectrograms from them, but at that point we're creating an awful lot of data that we will need to mix together at runtime. Thankfully, we can do some transformations on the spectrograms themselves.

SpecAugment

Now, you might be thinking at this point: "Wait, these spectrograms are just images! We can use any image transform we want on them!" And yes! Gold star for you in the back. But we do have to be a little careful; it's possible, for example, that a random crop may cut out enough frequencies that it potentially changes the output class. This is much less of an issue in our ESC-50 dataset, but if you were doing something like speech recognition, that would definitely be something you'd have to consider when applying augmentations. Another intriguing possibility is that because we know that all the spectrograms have the same structure (they're always going to be a frequency graph!), we could create image-based transforms that work specifically around that structure.

In 2019, Google released a paper on SpecAugment,[3] which reported new state-of-the-art results on many audio datasets. The team obtained these results by using three new data augmentation techniques that they applied directly to a mel spectrogram: time warping, frequency masking, and time masking. We won't look at time warping because the benefit derived from it is small, but we'll implement custom transforms for masking time and frequency.

Frequency masking

Frequency masking randomly removes a frequency or set of frequencies from our audio input. This attempts to make the model work harder; it cannot simply *memorize* an input and its class, because the input will have different frequencies masked during each batch. The model will instead have to learn other features that can determine how to map the input to a class, which hopefully should result in a more accurate model.

In our mel spectrograms, this is shown by making sure that nothing appears in the spectrograph for that frequency at any time step. Figure 6-7 shows what this looks like: essentially, a blank line drawn across a natural spectrogram.

Here's the code for a custom `Transform` that implements frequency masking:

```
class FrequencyMask(object):
    """
    Example:
      >>> transforms.Compose([
      >>>     transforms.ToTensor(),
      >>>     FrequencyMask(max_width=10, use_mean=False),
      >>> ])
```

---

3 See "SpecAugment: A Simple Data Augmentation Method for Automatic Speech Recognition" (*https://arxiv.org/abs/1904.08779*) by Daniel S. Park et al. (2019).

```
    """

    def __init__(self, max_width, use_mean=True):
        self.max_width = max_width
        self.use_mean = use_mean

    def __call__(self, tensor):
        """
        Args:
            tensor (Tensor): Tensor image of
            size (C, H, W) where the frequency
            mask is to be applied.

        Returns:
            Tensor: Transformed image with Frequency Mask.
        """
        start = random.randrange(0, tensor.shape[2])
        end = start + random.randrange(1, self.max_width)
        if self.use_mean:
            tensor[:, start:end, :] = tensor.mean()
        else:
            tensor[:, start:end, :] = 0
        return tensor

    def __repr__(self):
        format_string = self.__class__.__name__ + "(max_width="
        format_string += str(self.max_width) + ")"
        format_string += 'use_mean=' + (str(self.use_mean) + ')')

        return format_string
```

When the transform is applied, PyTorch will call the __call__ method with the tensor representation of the image (so we need to place it in a Compose chain after the image has been converted to a tensor, not before). We're assuming that the tensor will be in *channels × height × width* format, and we want to set the height values in a small range, to either zero or the mean of the image (because we're using log mel spectrograms, the mean should be the same as zero, but we include both options so you can experiment to see if one works better than the other). The range is provided by the max_width parameter, and our resulting pixel mask will be between 1 and max_pixels wide. We also need to pick a random starting point for the mask, which is what the start variable is for. Finally, the complicated part of this transform—we apply our generated mask:

```
tensor[:, start:end, :] = tensor.mean()
```

This isn't quite so bad when we break it down. Our tensor has three dimensions, but we want to apply this transform across all the red, green, and blue channels, so we use the bare : to select everything in that dimension. Using start:end, we select our height range, and then we select everything in the width channel, as we want to apply our mask across every time step. And then on the righthand side of the expression, we set the value; in this case, `tensor.mean()`. If we take a random tensor from the ESC-50 dataset and apply the transform to it, we can see in Figure 6-7 that this class is creating the required mask.

```
torchvision.transforms.Compose([FrequencyMask(max_width=10, use_mean=False),
torchvision.transforms.ToPILImage()])(torch.rand(3,250,200))
```

Figure 6-7. Frequency mask applied to a random ESC-50 sample

Next we'll turn our attention to time masking.

Time masking

With our frequency mask complete, we can turn to the *time mask*, which does the same as the frequency mask, but in the time domain. The code here is mostly the same:

```
class TimeMask(object):
    """
    Example:
        >>> transforms.Compose([
        >>>     transforms.ToTensor(),
        >>>     TimeMask(max_width=10, use_mean=False),
        >>> ])

    """

    def __init__(self, max_width, use_mean=True):
        self.max_width = max_width
        self.use_mean = use_mean

    def __call__(self, tensor):
        """
        Args:
            tensor (Tensor): Tensor image of
            size (C, H, W) where the time mask
            is to be applied.

        Returns:
            Tensor: Transformed image with Time Mask.
        """
        start = random.randrange(0, tensor.shape[1])
        end = start + random.randrange(0, self.max_width)
        if self.use_mean:
```

```
        tensor[:, :, start:end] = tensor.mean()
    else:
        tensor[:, :, start:end] = 0
    return tensor

def __repr__(self):
    format_string = self.__class__.__name__ + "(max_width="
    format_string += str(self.max_width) + ")"
    format_string += 'use_mean=' + (str(self.use_mean) + ')')
    return format_string
```

As you can see, this class is similar to the frequency mask. The only difference is that our `start` variable now ranges at some point on the height axis, and when we're doing our masking, we do this:

```
tensor[:, :, start:end] = 0
```

This indicates that we select all the values of the first two dimensions of our tensor and the `start:end` range in the last dimension. And again, we can apply this to a random tensor from ESC-50 to see that the mask is being applied correctly, as shown in Figure 6-8.

```
torchvision.transforms.Compose([TimeMask(max_width=10, use_mean=False),
torchvision.transforms.ToPILImage()])(torch.rand(3,250,200))
```

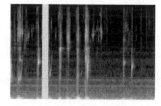

Figure 6-8. Time mask applied to a random ESC-50 sample

To finish our augmentation, we create a new wrapper transformation that ensures that one or both of the masks is applied to a spectrogram image:

```
class PrecomputedTransformESC50(Dataset):
    def __init__(self,path,dpi=50):
        files = Path(path).glob('{}*.wav.png'.format(dpi))
        self.items = [(f,f.name.split("-")[-1].replace(".wav.png",""))
                    for f in files]
        self.length = len(self.items)
        self.transforms = transforms.Compose([
    transforms.ToTensor(),
    RandomApply([FrequencyMask(self.max_freqmask_width)]p=0.5),
    RandomApply([TimeMask(self.max_timemask_width)]p=0.5)
])

    def __getitem__(self, index):
        filename, label = self.items[index]
```

```
        img = Image.open(filename)
        return (self.transforms(img), label)

    def __len__(self):
        return self.length
```

Try rerunning the training loop with this data augmentation and see if you, like Google, achieve better accuracy with these masks. But maybe there's still more that we can try with this dataset?

Further Experiments

So far, we've created two neural networks—one based on the raw audio waveform, and the other based on the images of mel spectrograms—to classify sounds from the ESC-50 dataset. Although you've seen that the ResNet-powered model is more accurate using the power of transfer learning, it would be an interesting experiment to create a combination of the two networks to see whether that increases or decreases the accuracy. A simple way of doing this would be to revisit the ensembling approach from Chapter 4: just combine and average the predictions. Also, we skipped over the idea of building a network based on the raw data we were getting from the spectrograms. If a model is created that works on that data, does it help overall accuracy if it is introduced to the ensemble? We can also use other versions of ResNet, or we could create new architectures that use different pretrained models such as VGG or Inception as a backbone. Explore some of these options and see what happens; in my experiments, SpecAugment improves ESC-50 classification accuracy by around 2%.

Conclusion

In this chapter, we used two very different strategies for audio classification, took a brief tour of PyTorch's torchaudio library, and saw how to precompute transformations on datasets when doing transformations on the fly would have a severe impact on training time. We discussed two approaches to data augmentation. As an unexpected bonus, we again stepped through how to train an image-based model by using transfer learning to quickly generate a classifier with decent accuracy compared to the others on the ESC-50 leaderboard.

This wraps up our tour through images, test, and audio, though we return to all three in Chapter 9 when we look at some applications that use PyTorch. Next up, though, we look at how to debug models when they're not training quite right or fast enough.

Further Reading

- "Interpreting and Explaining Deep Neural Networks for Classification of Audio Signals" (*https://arxiv.org/abs/1807.03418*) by Sören Becker et al. (2018)
- "CNN Architectures for Large-Scale Audio Classification" (*https://arxiv.org/abs/1609.09430v2*) by Shawn Hershey et al. (2016)

CHAPTER 7

Debugging PyTorch Models

We've created a lot of models so far in this book, but in this chapter, we have a brief look at interpreting them and working out what's going on underneath the covers. We take a look at using class activation mapping with PyTorch hooks to determine the focus of a model's decision about how to connect PyTorch to Google's TensorBoard for debugging purposes. I show how to use flame graphs to identify the bottlenecks in transforms and training pipelines, as well as provide a worked example of speeding up a slow transformation. Finally, we look at how to trade compute for memory when working with larger models using *checkpointing*. First, though, a brief word about your data.

It's 3 a.m. What Is Your Data Doing?

Before we delve into all the shiny things like TensorBoard or gradient checkpointing to use massive models on a single GPU, ask yourself this: do you understand your data? If you're classifying inputs, do you have a balanced sample across all the available labels? In the training, validation, and test sets?

And furthermore, are you sure your labels are *right*? Important image-based datasets such as MNIST and CIFAR-10 (Canadian Institute for Advanced Research) are known to contain some incorrect labels. You should check yours, especially if categories are similar to one another, like dog breeds or plant varieties. Simply doing a sanity check of your data may end up saving a lot of time if you discover that, say, one category of labels has only tiny images, whereas all the others have large-resolution examples.

Once you've made sure your data is in good condition, then yes, let's head over to TensorBoard to start checking out some possible issues in your model.

TensorBoard

TensorBoard is a web application designed for visualizing various aspects of neural networks. It allows for easy, real-time viewing of statistics such as accuracy, losses activation values, and really anything you want to send across the wire. Although it was written with TensorFlow in mind, it has such an agnostic and fairly straightforward API that working with it in PyTorch is not that different from how you'd use it in TensorFlow. Let's install it and see how we can use it to gain some insights about our models.

 When reading up on PyTorch, you'll likely come across references to an application called Visdom (*https://oreil.ly/rZqv2*), which is Facebook's alternative to TensorBoard. Before PyTorch v1.1, the way to support visualizations was to use Visdom with PyTorch while third-party libraries such as `tensorboardX` were available to integrate with TensorBoard. While Visdom continues be maintained, the inclusion of an official TensorBoard integration in v1.1 and above suggests that the developers of PyTorch have recognized that TensorBoard is the de facto neural net visualizer tool.

Installing TensorBoard

Installing TensorBoard can be done with either `pip` or `conda`:

```
pip install tensorboard
conda install tensorboard
```

 PyTorch requires v1.14 or above of TensorBoard.

TensorBoard can then be started on the command line:

```
tensorboard --logdir=runs
```

You can then go to *http://[your-machine]:6006*, where you'll see the welcome screen shown in Figure 7-1. We can now send data to the application.

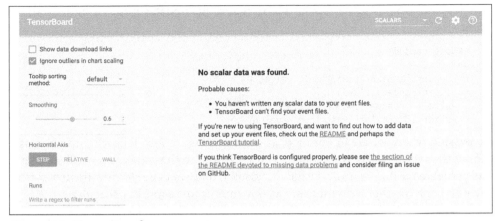

Figure 7-1. TensorBoard

Sending Data to TensorBoard

The module for using TensorBoard with PyTorch is located in `torch.utils.tensor` `board`:

```
from torch.utils.tensorboard import SummaryWriter
writer = SummaryWriter()
writer.add_scalar('example', 3)
```

We use the `SummaryWriter` class to talk to TensorBoard using the standard location for logging output, *./runs*, and we can send a scalar by using `add_scalar` with a tag. Because `SummaryWriter` works asynchronously, it may take a moment, but you should see TensorBoard update as shown in Figure 7-2.

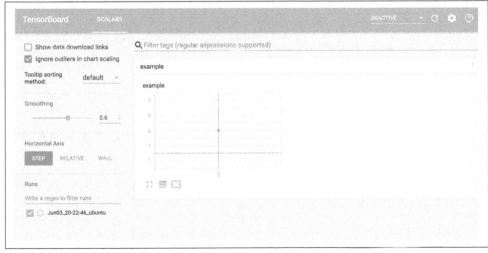

Figure 7-2. Example data point in TensorBoard

Not very exciting, is it? Let's write a loop that sends updates from an initial starting point:

```
import random
value = 10
writer.add_scalar('test_loop', value, 0)
for i in range(1,10000):
  value += random.random() - 0.5
  writer.add_scalar('test_loop', value, i)
```

By passing where we are in our loop, as shown in Figure 7-3, TensorBoard gives us a plot of the random walk we're doing from 10. If we run the code again, we'll see that it has generated a different *run* inside the display, and we can select on the left side of the web page whether we want to see all our runs or just some in particular.

Figure 7-3. Plotting a random walk in TensorBoard

We can use this to replace our `print` statements in the training loop. We can also send the model itself to get a representation in TensorBoard!

```
import torch
import torchvision
from torch.utils.tensorboard import SummaryWriter
from torchvision import datasets, transforms,models

writer = SummaryWriter()
model = models.resnet18(False)
writer.add_graph(model,torch.rand([1,3,224,224]))
```

```
def train(model, optimizer, loss_fn, train_data_loader, test_data_loader, epochs=20):
    model = model.train()
    iteration = 0

    for epoch in range(epochs):
        model.train()
        for batch in train_loader:
            optimizer.zero_grad()
            input, target = batch
            output = model(input)
            loss = loss_fn(output, target)
            writer.add_scalar('loss', loss, epoch)
            loss.backward()
            optimizer.step()

        model.eval()
        num_correct = 0
        num_examples = 0
        for batch in val_loader:
            input, target = batch
            output = model(input)
            correct = torch.eq(torch.max(F.softmax(output), dim=1)[1], target).view(-1)
            num_correct += torch.sum(correct).item()
            num_examples += correct.shape[0]
            print("Epoch {}, accuracy = {:.2f}".format(epoch,
                    num_correct / num_examples)
            writer.add_scalar('accuracy', num_correct / num_examples, epoch)
        iterations += 1
```

When it comes to using add_graph(), we need to send in a tensor to trace through
the model as well as the model itself. Once that happens, though, you should see
GRAPHS appear in TensorBoard, and as shown in Figure 7-4, clicking the large ResNet
block reveals further detail of the model's structure.

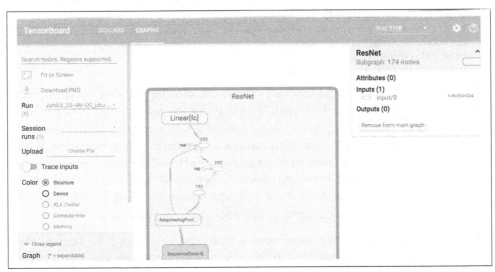

Figure 7-4. Visualizing ResNet

We now have the ability to send accuracy and loss information as well as model structure to TensorBoard. By aggregating multiple runs of accuracy and loss information, we can see whether anything is different in a particular run compared to others, which is a useful clue when trying to work out why a training run produced poor results. We return to TensorBoard shortly, but first let's look at other features that PyTorch makes available for debugging.

PyTorch Hooks

PyTorch has *hooks*, which are functions that can be attached to either a tensor or a module on the forward or backward pass. When PyTorch encounters a module with a hook during a pass, it will call the registered hooks. A hook registered on a tensor will be called when its gradient is being calculated.

Hooks are potentially powerful ways of manipulating modules and tensors because you can completely replace the output of what comes into the hook if you so desire. You could change the gradient, mask off activations, replace all the biases in the module, and so on. In this chapter, though, we're just going to use them as a way of obtaining information about the network as data flows through.

Given a ResNet-18 model, we can attach a forward hook on a particular part of the model by using `register_forward_hook`:

```
def print_hook(self, module, input, output):
  print(f"Shape of input is {input.shape}")

model = models.resnet18()
hook_ref  = model.fc.register_forward_hook(print_hook)
model(torch.rand([1,3,224,224]))
hook_ref.remove()
model(torch.rand([1,3,224,224]))
```

If you run this code you should see text printed out showing the shape of the input to the linear classifier layer of the model. Note that the second time you pass a random tensor through the model, you shouldn't see the `print` statement. When we add a hook to a module or tensor, PyTorch returns a reference to that hook. We should always save that reference (here we do it in `hook_ref`) and then call `remove()` when we're finished. If you don't store the reference, then it will just hang out and take up valuable memory (and potentially waste compute resources during a pass). Backward hooks work in the same way, except you call `register_backward_hook()` instead.

Of course, if we can `print()` something, we can certainly send it to TensorBoard! Let's see how to use both hooks and TensorBoard to get important stats on our layers during training.

Plotting Mean and Standard Deviation

To start, we set up a function that will send the mean and standard deviation of an output layer to TensorBoard:

```
def send_stats(i, module, input, output):
  writer.add_scalar(f"{i}-mean",output.data.std())
  writer.add_scalar(f"{i}-stddev",output.data.std())
```

We can't use this by itself to set up a forward hook, but using the Python function `partial()`, we can create a series of forward hooks that will attach themselves to a layer with a set `i` value that will make sure that the correct values are routed to the right graphs in TensorBoard:

```
from functools import partial

for i,m in enumerate(model.children()):
  m.register_forward_hook(partial(send_stats, i))
```

Note that we're using `model.children()`, which will attach only to each top-level block of the model, so if we have an `nn.Sequential()` layer (which we will have in a ResNet-based model), we'll attach a hook to only that block and not one for each individual module within the `nn.Sequential` list.

If we train our model with our usual training function, we should see the activations start streaming into TensorBoard, as shown in Figure 7-5. You'll have to switch to wall-clock time within the UI as we're no longer sending *step* information back to TensorBoard with the hook (as we're getting the module information only when the PyTorch hook is called).

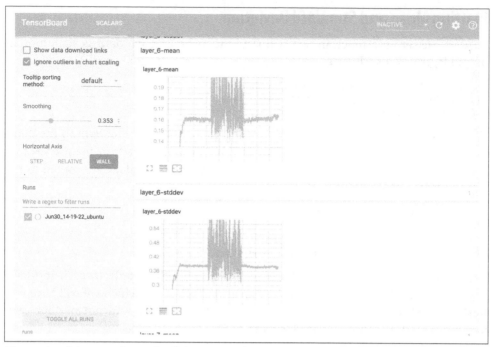

Figure 7-5. Mean and standard deviation of modules in TensorBoard

Now, I mentioned in Chapter 2 that, ideally, layers in a neural network should have a mean of 0 and a standard deviation of 1 to make sure that our calculations don't run off to infinity or to zero. Have a look at the layers in TensorBoard. Do they look like they're remaining in that value range? Does the plot sometimes spike and then collapse? If so, that could be a signal that the network is having difficulty training. In Figure 7-5, our mean is close to zero, but our standard deviation is also pretty close to zero as well. If this is happening in many layers of your network, it may be a sign that your activation functions (e.g., ReLU) are not quite suited to your problem domain. It might be worth experimenting with other functions to see if they improve the model's performance; PyTorch's LeakyReLU is a good alternative offering similar activations to the standard ReLU but lets more information through, which might help in training.

That about wraps up our look at TensorBoard, but the "Further Reading" on page 136 will point you to more resources. In the meantime, let's see how we can get a model to explain how it came to a decision.

Class Activation Mapping

Class activation mapping (CAM) is a technique for visualizing the activations of a network after it has classified an incoming tensor. In image-based classifiers, it's often shown as a heatmap on top of the original image, as shown in Figure 7-6.

Figure 7-6. Class activation mapping with Casper

From the heatmap, we can get an intuitive idea of how the network reached the decision of *Persian Cat* from the available ImageNet classes. The activations of the network are at their highest around the face and body of the cat and low elsewhere in the image.

To generate the heatmap, we capture the activations of the final convolutional layer of a network, just before it goes into the `Linear` layer, as this allows us to see what the combined CNN layers thinks are important as we head into the final mapping from image to classes. Thankfully, with PyTorch's hook feature, this is fairly straightforward. We wrap up the hook in a class, `SaveActivations`:

```
class SaveActivations():
    activations=None
    def __init__(self, m):
      self.hook = m.register_forward_hook(self.hook_fn)
    def hook_fn(self, module, input, output):
      self.features = output.data
    def remove(self):
      self.hook.remove()
```

We then push our image of Casper through the network (normalizing for ImageNet), apply `softmax` to turn the output tensor into probabilities, and use `torch.topk()` as a way of pulling out both the max probability and its index:

```
import torch
from torchvision import models, transforms
from torch.nn import functional as F

casper = Image.open("casper.jpg")
# Imagenet mean/std

normalize = transforms.Normalize(
    mean=[0.485, 0.456, 0.406],
    std=[0.229, 0.224, 0.225]
)
```

```
preprocess = transforms.Compose([
    transforms.Resize((224,224)),
    transforms.ToTensor(),
    normalize
])

display_transform = transforms.Compose([
    transforms.Resize((224,224))])

casper_tensor = preprocess(casper)

model = models.resnet18(pretrained=True)
model.eval()
casper_activations = SaveActivations(model.layer_4)
prediction = model(casper_tensor.unsqueeze(0))
pred_probabilities = F.softmax(prediction).data.squeeze()
casper_activations.remove()
torch.topk(pred_probabilities,1)
```

 I haven't explained torch.nn.functional yet, but the best way to think about it is that it contains the implementation of the *functions* provided in torch.nn. For example, if you create an instance of torch.nn.softmax(), you get an object with a forward() method that performs softmax. If you look in the actual source for torch.nn.softmax(), you'll see that all that method does is call F.softmax(). As we don't need softmax here to be part of a network, we're just calling the underlying function.

If we now access casper_activations.activations, we'll see that it has been populated by a tensor, which contains the activations of the final convolutional layer we need. We then do this:

```
fts = sf[0].features[idx]
        prob = np.exp(to_np(log_prob))
        preds = np.argmax(prob[idx])
        fts_np = to_np(fts)
        f2=np.dot(np.rollaxis(fts_np,0,3), prob[idx])
        f2-=f2.min()
        f2/=f2.max()
        f2
plt.imshow(dx)
plt.imshow(scipy.misc.imresize(f2, dx.shape), alpha=0.5, cmap='jet');
```

This calculates the dot product of the activations from Casper (we index into 0 because of the batching in the first dimension of the input tensor, remember). As mentioned in Chapter 1, PyTorch stores image data in C × H × W format, so we next need to rearrange the dimensions back to H × W × C for displaying the image. We then remove the minimums from the tensor and scale by the maximum to ensure that we're focusing on only the highest activations in the resulting heatmap (i.e., what speaks to *Persian Cat*). Finally, we use some `matplot` magic to display Casper and then the tensor on top, resized and given a standard `jet` color map. Note that by replacing `idx` with a different class, you can see the heatmap indicating which activations (if any) are present in the image when classified. So if the model predicts *car*, you can see which parts of the image were used to make that decision. The second-highest probability for Casper is *Angora Rabbit*, and we can see from the CAM for that index that it focused on his very fluffy fur!

That wraps up our look into what a model is doing when it makes a decision. Next, we're going to investigate what a model spends most of its time doing while it's in a training loop or during inference.

Flame Graphs

In contrast to TensorBoard, *flame graphs* weren't created specifically for neural networks. Nope, not even TensorFlow. In fact, flame graphs trace their origin back to 2011, when an engineer named Brendan Gregg, working at a company called Joyent, came up with the technique to help debug an issue he was having with MySQL. The idea was to take massive stacktraces and turn them into a single image, which by itself delivers a picture of what is happening on a CPU over a period of time.

 Brendan Gregg now works for Netflix and has a huge amount of performance-related work available to read and digest (*http:// www.brendangregg.com*).

Using an example of MySQL inserting a row into a table, we sample the *stack* hundreds or thousand of times a second. Each time we sample, we get a *stacktrace* that shows us all the functions in the stack at that point in time. So if we are in a function that has been called by another function, we'll get a trace that includes both the callee and caller functions. A sample trace looks like this:

```
65.00%     0.00%  mysqld    [kernel.kallsyms]    [k] entry_SYSCALL_64_fastpath
             |
           ---entry_SYSCALL_64_fastpath
              |
              |--18.75%-- sys_io_getevents
              |           read_events
              |           schedule
              |           __schedule
              |           finish_task_switch
              |
              |--10.00%-- sys_fsync
              |           do_fsync
```

```
        |              vfs_fsync_range
        |              ext4_sync_file
        |              |
        |              |--8.75%-- jbd2_complete_transaction
        |              |          jbd2_log_wait_commit
        |              |          |
        |              |          |--6.25%-- _cond_resched
        |              |          |          preempt_schedule_common
        |              |          |          __schedule
```

There's a *lot* of this information; that's just a tiny sample of a 400KB set of stack traces. Even with this collation (which may not be present in all stacktraces), it's difficult to see what's going on here.

The flame graph version, on the other hand, is simple and clear, as you can see in Figure 7-7. The y-axis is stack height, and the x-axis is, while *not time*, a representation of how often that function is on the stack when it has been sampled. So if we had a function at the top of the stack that was covering, say, 80% of the graph, we'd know that the program is spending an awful lot of running time in that function and that maybe we should look at the function to see just what is making it take so long.

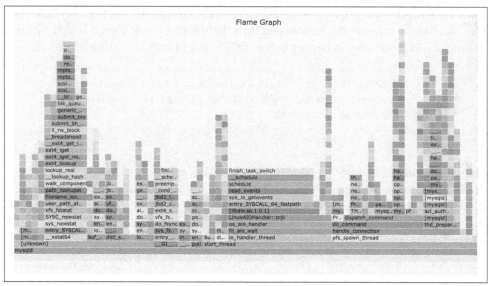

Figure 7-7. MySQL flame graph

You might ask, "What does this have to do with deep learning?" Fair enough; it's a common trope in deep learning research that when training slows down, you just buy another 10 GPUs or give Google a lot more money for TPU pods. But maybe your training pipeline isn't GPU bound after all. Perhaps you have a really slow transformation, and when you get all those shiny new graphics cards, they don't end up helping as much as you'd have thought. Flame graphs provide a simple, at-a-glance way of identifying CPU-bound bottlenecks, and these often occur in practical deep learning solutions. For example, remember all those image-based transforms we talked about in Chapter 4? Most of them use the Python Imaging Library and are totally CPU bound. With large datasets, you'll be doing those transforms over and over again within the training loop! So while they're not often brought up in the context of deep learning, flame graphs are a great tool to have in your box. If nothing else, you can use them as evidence to your boss that you really are GPU bound and you need all those TPU credits by next Thursday! We'll look at getting flame graphs from your training cycles and at fixing a slow transformation by moving it from the CPU to the GPU.

Installing py-spy

There are many ways to generate the stacktraces that can be turned into flame graphs. The one in the previous section was generated using the Linux tool perf, which is a complex and powerful tool. We'll take a somewhat easier option and use py-spy, a Rust-based stack profiler, to directly generate flame graphs. Install it via pip:

```
pip install py-spy
```

You can find the process identifier (PID) of a running process and attach py-spy by using a --pid argument:

```
py-spy --flame profile.svg --pid 12345
```

Or you can pass in a Python script, which is how we run it in this chapter. First, let's run it on a simple Python script:

```
import torch
import torchvision

def get_model():
    return torchvision.models.resnet18(pretrained=True)

def get_pred(model):
    return model(torch.rand([1,3,224,224]))

model = get_model()

for i in range(1,10000):
    get_pred(model)
```

Save this as *flametest.py* and let's run py-spy on it, sampling 99 times a second and running for 30 seconds:

```
py-spy -r 99 -d 30 --flame profile.svg -- python t.py
```

Open the *profile.svg* file in your browser, and let's take a look at the resulting graph.

Reading Flame Graphs

Figure 7-8 shows what the graph should look like, roughly speaking (because of sampling, it may not look exactly like this on your machine). The first thing you'll probably notice is that the graph is going down instead of up. py-spy writes out flame graphs in *icicle* format, so the stack looks like stalactites instead of the flames of the classic flame graph. I prefer the normal format, but py-spy doesn't give us the option to change it, and it doesn't make that much difference.

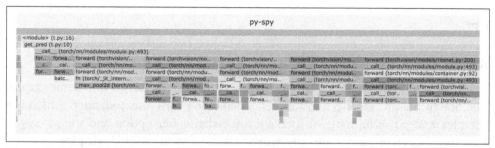

Figure 7-8. Flame graph on ResNet loading and inference

At a glance, you should see that most of the execution time is spent in various for ward() calls, which makes sense because we are making lots of predictions with the model. What about those tiny blocks on the left? If you click them, you should find that the SVG file zooms in as shown in Figure 7-9.

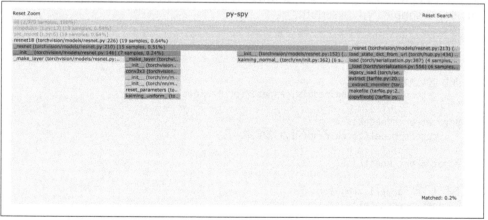

Figure 7-9. Zoomed flame graph

Here, we can see the script setting up the ResNet-18 module and also calling load_state_dict() to load the saved weights from disk (because we called it with pretrained=True). You can click Reset Zoom to go back to the full flame graph. Also, a search bar on the right will highlight matching bars in purple, if you're trying to hunt down a function. Try it with *resnet*, and it'll show you every function call on the stack with *resnet* in its name. This can be useful for finding functions that aren't on the stack much or seeing how much that pattern appears in the graph overall.

Play around with the SVG for a bit and see how much CPU time things like Batch-Norm and pooling are taking up in this toy example. Next, we'll look at a way to use flame graphs to find an issue, fix it, and verify it with another flame graph.

Fixing a Slow Transformation

In real-world situations, part of your data pipeline may be causing a slowdown. This is a particular problem if you have a slow transformation, as it will be called many times during a training batch, causing a massive bottleneck in creating your model. Here's an example transformation pipeline and a data loader:

```
import torch
import torchvision
from torch import optim
import torch.nn as nn
from torchvision import datasets, transforms, models
import torch.utils.data
from PIL import Image
import numpy as np

device = "cuda:0"
model = models.resnet18(pretrained=True)
model.to(device)


class BadRandom(object):
    def __call__(self, img):
        img_np = np.array(img)
        random = np.random.random_sample(img_np.shape)
        out_np = img_np + random
        out = Image.fromarray(out_np.astype('uint8'), 'RGB')
        return out

    def __repr__(self):
        str = f"{self.__class__.__name__ }"
        return str

train_data_path = "catfish/train"
image_transforms =
torchvision.transforms.Compose(
    [transforms.Resize((224,224)),BadRandom(), transforms.ToTensor()])
```

We're not going to run a full training loop; instead, we simulate 10 epochs of just pulling the images from the training data loader:

```
train_data = torchvision.datasets.ImageFolder(root=train_data_path,
transform=image_transforms)
```

```
batch_size=32
train_data_loader = torch.utils.data.DataLoader(train_data,
batch_size=batch_size)

optimizer = optim.Adam(model.parameters(), lr=2e-2)
criterion = nn.CrossEntropyLoss()

def train(model, optimizer, loss_fn,  train_loader, val_loader,
epochs=20, device='cuda:0'):
    model.to(device)
    for epoch in range(epochs):
        print(f"epoch {epoch}")
        model.train()
        for batch in train_loader:
            optimizer.zero_grad()
            ww, target = batch
            ww = ww.to(device)
            target= target.to(device)
            output = model(ww)
            loss = loss_fn(output, target)
            loss.backward()
            optimizer.step()

        model.eval()
        num_correct = 0
        num_examples = 0
        for batch in val_loader:
            input, target = batch
            input = input.to(device)
            target= target.to(device)
            output = model(input)
            correct = torch.eq(torch.max(output, dim=1)[1], target).view(-1)
            num_correct += torch.sum(correct).item()
            num_examples += correct.shape[0]
        print("Epoch {}, accuracy = {:.2f}"
        .format(epoch, num_correct / num_examples))

train(model,optimizer,criterion,
train_data_loader,train_data_loader,epochs=10)
```

Let's run that code under py-spy as before:

```
py-spy -r 99 -d 120 --flame slowloader.svg -- python slowloader.py
```

If you open the resulting *slowloader.svg*, you should hopefully see something like Figure 7-10. Although the flame graph is mostly occupied with loading the images and converting them to tensors, we are spending 16.87% of the sampled runtime in applying random noise. Looking at the code, our implementation of BadRandom is applying noise at the PIL stage rather than at the tensor stage, so we're at the mercy of the imaging library and NumPy rather than PyTorch itself. So our first idea would likely be to rewrite the transform so that it operates on tensors instead of the PIL images. That's likely to be faster, but not always—and the important thing when making performance changes is always to measure everything.

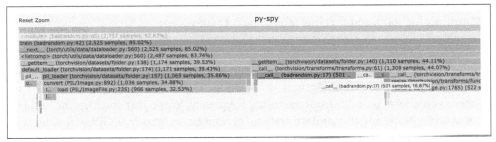

Figure 7-10. Flame graph with BadRandom

But here's a curious thing, which has been present all the way through the book, though I've not drawn attention to it until now: have you noticed that we pull batches from the data loader and then put those batches onto the GPU? Because the transforms occur as the loader gets batches from the dataset class, those transforms are always going to happen on the CPU. In some cases, that can lead to some crazy lateral thinking. We are applying random noise on every image. What if we could apply random noise on every image at once?

Here's the bit that might seem mind-bending at first: we're adding random noise to an image. We can write that as $x + y$, with x being our image and y our noise. We know that both image and noise are 3D (width, height, channels), so all we're doing here is matrix multiplication. And in a batch, we'll be doing this z times. We're just iterating over each image as we pull them out of the loader. But consider that at the end of the loading process, the images are transformed into tensors, a batch of $[z, c, h, w]$. Well, couldn't you just add a random tensor of shape $[z, c, h, w]$ and get the random noise applied that way? Instead of applying the noise in sequence, it happens all at once. We now have a matrix operation, and a very expensive GPU that just happens to be rather good at matrix operations. Try this in Jupyter Notebook to see the difference between CPU and GPU tensor matrix operations:

```
cpu_t1 = torch.rand(64,3,224,224)
cpu_t2 = torch.rand(64,3,224,224)
%timeit cpu_t1 + cpu_t2
>> 5.39 ms ± 4.29 µs per loop (mean ± std. dev. of 7 runs, 100 loops each)

gpu_t1 = torch.rand(64,3,224,224).to("cuda")
gpu_t2 = torch.rand(64,3,224,224).to("cuda")
%timeit gpu_t1 + gpu_t2
>> 297 µs ± 338 ns per loop (mean ± std. dev. of 7 runs, 10000 loops each)
```

That's just under 20 times faster. Instead of performing this transformation in our data loader, we can take it out and perform the matrix operations after we have the entire batch at our disposal:

```
def add_noise_gpu(tensor, device):
    random_noise = torch_rand_like(tensor).to(device)
    return tensor.add_(random_noise)
```

In our training loop, add this line after `input.to(device)`:

```
input = add_noise_gpu(input, device)
```

Then remove the `BadRandom` transform from the transform pipeline and test again with `py-spy`. The new flame graph is shown in Figure 7-11. It's so fast that it no longer even shows up under our sampling frequency. We've just sped up the code by almost 17%! Now, not all standard transforms can be written in a GPU-friendly way, but if it's possible and the transform is slowing you down, then it's definitely an option worth considering.

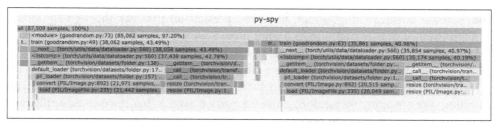

Figure 7-11. Flame graph with GPU-accelerated random noise

Now that we've considered compute, it's time to look at the other elephant in the room: memory, especially memory on the GPU.

Debugging GPU Issues

In this section, we drill down deeper into the GPU itself. One thing you'll soon discover in training larger deep learning models is that the shiny GPU that you've spent so much money on (or, more wisely, attached to a cloud-based instance) is brought to its knees regularly, bitterly complaining about running out of memory. But that GPU has gigabytes and gigabytes of storage! How could you possibly run out?

Models tend to soak up a lot of memory. ResNet-152, for example, has about 60 million activations, all of which take up precious space on your GPU. Let's see how to peer inside the GPU to determine what could be going on when you're running low on memory.

Checking Your GPU

Assuming you are using an NVIDIA GPU (check your alternate GPU supplier's drivers website for their own utilities if you're using something different), the CUDA installation includes a rather useful command-line tool called `nvidia-smi`. When run with no arguments, this tool can give you a snapshot of the memory being used on the GPU, and even better, what is using it! Figure 7-12 shows output from running `nvidia-smi` within the terminal. Within a notebook, you can call out to the utility by using `!nvidia-smi`.

```
ian@ubuntu:~/notebooks$ nvidia-smi
Fri Jun  7 10:27:32 2019
+-----------------------------------------------------------------------------+
| NVIDIA-SMI 396.54                 Driver Version: 396.54                     |
|-------------------------------+----------------------+----------------------+
| GPU  Name        Persistence-M| Bus-Id        Disp.A | Volatile Uncorr. ECC |
| Fan  Temp  Perf  Pwr:Usage/Cap|         Memory-Usage | GPU-Util  Compute M. |
|===============================+======================+======================|
|   0  GeForce GTX 108...  Off  | 00000000:01:00.0  On |                  N/A |
| 0%   26C    P8     9W / 250W |   8079MiB / 11176MiB |      0%      Default |
+-------------------------------+----------------------+----------------------+

+-----------------------------------------------------------------------------+
| Processes:                                                       GPU Memory |
|  GPU       PID   Type   Process name                             Usage      |
|=============================================================================|
|    0      2006      G   /usr/lib/xorg/Xorg                            32MiB |
|    0      2413      G   /usr/bin/gnome-shell                          58MiB |
|    0      3993      C   /home/ian/anaconda3/bin/python              1407MiB |
|    0     17301      C   /home/ian/anaconda3/bin/python               527MiB |
|    0     19205      C   /home/ian/anaconda3/bin/python               523MiB |
|    0     31226      C   /home/ian/anaconda3/bin/python               885MiB |
|    0     32113      C   /home/ian/anaconda3/bin/python              4633MiB |
+-----------------------------------------------------------------------------+
```

Figure 7-12. Output from nvidia-smi

This example is taken from my home machine running a 1080 Ti. I'm running a bunch of notebooks, each of which is taking up a chunk of memory, but one is using 4GB! You can get the current PID of a notebook by using `os.getpid()`. It turns out that the process using the most memory was actually an experimental notebook I was using to test out the GPU transforms in the previous section! You can imagine that with the model, batch data, and data for the forward and backward passes, things get tight memory-wise rather quickly.

 I also have a couple of processes running that are, perhaps surprisingly, doing graphics—namely, the X server and GNOME. Unless you've built a local machine, you almost certainly won't see these.

In addition, PyTorch will dedicate a chunk of memory to itself and CUDA per process that is around 0.5GB of memory. This means that it's a better idea to work on one project at a time and not leave Jupyter Notebook running all over the place as I have here (you can use the Kernel menu to shut down the Python process connected to a notebook).

Running `nvidia-smi` by itself will give you the current snapshot of the GPU's usage, but you can get continual output by using the `-l` flag. Here's an example command that will dump the timestamp, used memory, free memory, total memory, and GPU utilization every 5 seconds:

```
nvidia-smi --query-gpu=timestamp,
memory.used, memory.free,memory.total,utilization.gpu --format=csv -l 5
```

If you really think that your GPU is using up more memory than it should be, you can try getting Python's garbage collector involved. If you have a `ten sor_to_be_deleted` that you no longer need and want it gone from the GPU, then a tip from the bowels of the fast.ai library is to give it a shove with `del`:

```
import gc
del tensor_to_be_deleted
gc.collect()
```

If you're doing a lot of work inside Jupyter Notebook creating and re-creating models, you may find that deleting some references and invoking the garbage collector by using `gc.collect()` will claw back some memory. If you're still having trouble with memory, read on, because there may be an answer to your woes!

Gradient Checkpointing

Despite all the deletion and garbage collection tricks presented in the previous section, you might still find yourself running out of memory. The next thing to do for most applications is to reduce the batch size of data going through a model during the training loop. This will work, but you're going to increase training time for each epoch, and it's likely that the model will not be as good as an equivalent one trained with enough memory to handle the larger batch sizes, because you'll be seeing more of the dataset on every pass. However, we can trade compute against memory for large models in PyTorch by using *gradient checkpointing*.

One of the problems when dealing with bigger models is that the forward and backward passes create lots of intermediate state, all of which occupy GPU memory. The goal of gradient checkpointing is to reduce the amount of state that may be on the GPU at any one time by *segmenting* the model. This approach means that you can have between four and ten times the batch size with a nonsegmented model, with that being offset by the training being more compute-intensive. During the forward pass, PyTorch saves the inputs and the parameters to a segment, but doesn't actually do the forward pass itself. During the backward pass, these are retrieved by PyTorch, and the forward pass is computed for that segment. The intermediate values are passed onto the next segment, but those have to be performed on only a segment-by-segment basis.

Chopping up a model into these segments is handled by `torch.utils.check point.checkpoint_sequential()`. It works on `nn.Sequential` layers or generated lists of layers, with the proviso that they need to be in sequence of how they occur in the model. Here's how it would work on the `features` module in AlexNet:

```python
from torch.utils.checkpoint import checkpoint_sequential
import torch.nn as nn

class CheckpointedAlexNet(nn.Module):

    def __init__(self, num_classes=1000, chunks=2):
        super(CheckpointedAlexNet, self).__init__()
        self.features = nn.Sequential(
            nn.Conv2d(3, 64, kernel_size=11, stride=4, padding=2),
            nn.ReLU(inplace=True),
            nn.MaxPool2d(kernel_size=3, stride=2),
            nn.Conv2d(64, 192, kernel_size=5, padding=2),
            nn.ReLU(inplace=True),
            nn.MaxPool2d(kernel_size=3, stride=2),
            nn.Conv2d(192, 384, kernel_size=3, padding=1),
            nn.ReLU(inplace=True),
            nn.Conv2d(384, 256, kernel_size=3, padding=1),
            nn.ReLU(inplace=True),
            nn.Conv2d(256, 256, kernel_size=3, padding=1),
            nn.ReLU(inplace=True),
            nn.MaxPool2d(kernel_size=3, stride=2),
        )
        self.avgpool = nn.AdaptiveAvgPool2d((6, 6))
        self.classifier = nn.Sequential(
            nn.Dropout(),
            nn.Linear(256 * 6 * 6, 4096),
            nn.ReLU(inplace=True),
            nn.Dropout(),
            nn.Linear(4096, 4096),
            nn.ReLU(inplace=True),
            nn.Linear(4096, num_classes),
        )

    def forward(self, x):
        x = checkpoint_sequential(self.features, chunks, x)
        x = self.avgpool(x)
        x = x.view(x.size(0), 256 * 6 * 6)
        x = self.classifier(x)
        return x
```

As you can see, not much is different here, making checkpointing an easy addition to models when required. We've added a `chunks` parameter to the new version of the model, with the default being to split it into two segments. All we then need to do is make a call to `checkpoint_sequential` with the `features` module, the number of segments, and our inputs. And that's it!

One slight kink in checkpointing is that it doesn't behave well with `BatchNorm` or `Drop out` layers because of how they interact with the forward pass. To work around that, you can just checkpoint parts of the model before and after those layers. In our `Check pointedAlexNet`, we could perhaps break the `classifier` module into two parts: one containing the `Dropout` layers that are uncheckpointed, and a final `nn.Sequential` module containing our `Linear` layers that we could checkpoint in the same way we did with `features`.

If you find yourself with diminishing batch sizes in order to get a model to run, consider checkpointing before you ask for a larger GPU!

Conclusion

Hopefully, you're now equipped to go hunting in search of answers when training your model doesn't go as planned. From sanitizing data to running flame graph or TensorBoard visualizations, you have a lot of tools at your disposal; you've also seen ways of trading memory for compute with GPU transforms, and vice versa using checkpointing.

Armed with a properly trained, debugged model, we're on our way to that harshest of realms: *production*.

Further Reading

- TensorBoard documentation (*https://oreil.ly/MELKl*)
- TensorBoard GitHub (*https://oreil.ly/21bIM*)
- Fast.ai Lesson 10: Looking Inside The Model (*https://oreil.ly/K4dz-*)
- Investigation into BatchNorm within a ResNet model (*https://oreil.ly/EXdK3*)
- Deeper dive into generating flame graphs (*https://oreil.ly/4Ectg*) with Brendan Gregg
- nvidia-smi documentation (*https://oreil.ly/W1g0n*)
- PyTorch gradient checkpointing documentation (*https://oreil.ly/v0apy*)

CHAPTER 8

PyTorch in Production

Now that you've learned how to use PyTorch to classify images, text, and sound, the next step is to look at how to deploy PyTorch applications in production. In this chapter, we create applications that run inference on PyTorch models over HTTP and gRPC. We then package those applications into Docker containers and deploy them to a Kubernetes cluster running on Google Cloud.

In the second half, we look at TorchScript, a new technology introduced in PyTorch 1.0 that allows us to use just-in-time (JIT) tracing to produce optimized models that can be run from C++. We also have a brief look at how to compress models with quantization. First up, let's look at model serving.

Model Serving

We've spent the last six chapters building models in PyTorch, but building a model is only part of building a deep learning application. After all, a model may have amazing accuracy (or other relevant metric), but if it never makes any predictions, is it worth anything? What we want is an easy way to package our models so they can respond to requests (either over the web or other means, as we'll see) and can be run in production with the minimum of effort.

Thankfully, Python allows us to get a web service up and running quickly with the Flask framework. In this section, we build a simple service that loads our ResNet-based *cat or fish* model, accepts requests that include an image URL, and returns a JSON response that indicates whether the image contains a cat or a fish.

What happens if we send the model a picture of a dog? The model will tell you that it is either a fish or a cat. It has no concept of anything but the available choices and will always pick one. Some deep learning practitioners add an extra class, Unknown, during training and throw in labeled examples that aren't any of the required classes. This works to a certain extent, but it essentially tries to make the neural net learn *everything that isn't a cat or fish*, which is difficult for you and me to express, let alone a series of matrix calculations! Another option is to look at the probability output generated by the final softmax. If the model is producing a prediction that is roughly 50/50 cat/fish or spread out across your classes, then maybe suggest Unknown.

Building a Flask Service

Let's get a web service-enabled version of our model up and running. *Flask* is a popular framework for creating web services with Python, and we'll be using it as a base throughout this chapter. Install the Flask library with either pip or conda:

```
conda install -c anaconda flask
pip install flask
```

Create a new directory called *catfish* and copy your model definition inside as *model.py*:

```
from torchvision import models

CatfishClasses = ["cat","fish"]

CatfishModel = models.ResNet50()
CatfishModel.fc = nn.Sequential(nn.Linear(transfer_model.fc.in_features,500),
                    nn.ReLU(),
                    nn.Dropout(), nn.Linear(500,2))
```

Note that we do not specify a pretrained model here, because we will be loading our saved weights in the Flask server startup process. Then create another Python script, *catfish_server.py*, where we will start our web service:

```
from flask import Flask, jsonify
from . import CatfishModel
from torchvision import transforms
import torch
import os

def load_model():
  return model

app = Flask(__name__)

@app.route("/")
```

```
def status():
  return jsonify({"status": "ok"})

@app.route("/predict", methods=['GET', 'POST'])
def predict():
  img_url = request.image_url
  img_tensor = open_image(BytesIO(response.content))
  prediction = model(img_tensor)
  predicted_class = CatfishClasses[torch.argmax(prediction)]
  return jsonify({"image": img_url, "prediction": predicted_class})

if __name__ == '__main__':
  app.run(host=os.environ["CATFISH_HOST"], port=os.environ["CATFISH_PORT"])
```

You can start up a web server on the command line by setting the CATFISH_HOST and CATFISH_PORT environment variables:

```
CATFISH_HOST=127.0.0.1 CATFISH_PORT=8080 python catfish_server.py
```

If you point your web browser at *http://127.0.0.1:8080*, you should get a status: "ok" JSON response as shown in Figure 8-1.

Figure 8-1. OK response from CATFISH

We discuss this in more detail later in this chapter, but don't deploy a Flask service directly to production because the built-in server is not adequate for production usage.

To make a prediction, find an image URL and send it as a GET request with the image_url parameter to the /predict path. You should see a JSON response showing the URL and the predicted class, as shown in Figure 8-2.

Figure 8-2. Prediction from CATFISH

The magic in Flask is in the `@app.route()` annotations. These allow us to attach normal Python functions that will be run when a user hits a particular endpoint. In our `predict()` method, we pull out the `img_url` parameter from either a GET or POST HTTP request, open that URL as a PIL image, and push it through a simple `torchvision` transform pipeline to resize it and turn the image into a tensor.

This gives us a tensor of shape `[3,224,224]`, but because of the way our model works, we need to turn it into a batch of size 1—that is, `[1,3,224,224]`. So we use `unsqueeze()` again to expand our tensor by inserting a new empty axis in front of the existing dimensions. We can then pass it through the model as usual, which gives us our prediction tensor. As we have done previously, we use `torch.argmax()` to find the element of the tensor with the highest value and use that to index into the `CatfishClasses` array. Finally, we return a JSON response with the name of the class and the image URL we performed the prediction on.

If you experiment with the server at this point, you might be a little disappointed with the classification performance. Didn't we spend a lot of time training it? Yes, we did, but in re-creating the model, we have simply created a set of layers with the standard PyTorch initialization! So no wonder it's not good. Let's flesh out `load_model()` to load in our parameters.

 We're returning only the predicted class here, not the complete set of predictions across all classes. You could certainly return the prediction tensor as well, though be aware that the complete tensor output makes it a little easier for attackers to build up a replica of your model through more *information leakage*.

Setting Up the Model Parameters

In Chapter 2, we talked about the two ways to save a model after training, either by writing the entire model to disk with `torch.save()` or by saving the `state_dict()` of all the weights and biases of the model (but not the structure). For our production-based service, we need to load in an already-trained model, so what should we use?

In my opinion, you should go for the `state_dict` approach. Saving the entire model is an attractive option, but you will become incredibly sensitive to any changes in the model structure or even the directory structure of the training setup. That's likely to cause a problem with loading it up in a separate service that runs elsewhere. If we're making a migration to a slightly different layout, we'd like to not have to rework everything.

We'd also be better off not hardcoding the filename of the saved `state_dicts()` so we can decouple model updates from our service. This means we can restart the service with a new model or revert to an earlier model with ease. We pass in the filename as a parameter—but where should it point? For the moment, assume that we can set an environment variable called CATFISH_MODEL_LOCATION, and use that in load_model():

```
def load_model():
  m = CatfishModel()
  location = os.environ["CATFISH_MODEL_LOCATION"]
  m.load_state_dict(torch.load(location))
  return m
```

Now, copy in one of the model weight files you saved in Chapter 4 into the directory and set CATFISH_MODEL_LOCATION to point to that file:

```
export CATFISH_MODEL_LOCATION=catfishweights.pt
```

Restart the server, and you should see that the service is a lot more accurate!

We now have a working minimal web service (you'd probably want a little more error handling, but I'm leaving that as an exercise for you!). But how do we get that running on a server in, say, AWS or Google Cloud? Or just on somebody else's laptop? After all, we have installed a bunch of libraries to get this working. We can use Docker to package everything up into one *container* that can be installed in any Linux (or Windows, with the new Windows Subsystem for Linux!) environment in seconds.

Building the Docker Container

Docker has become one of the de facto standards for application packaging in the past few years. Cutting-edge cluster environments such as Kubernetes have Docker at their core for deploying applications (as you'll see later in the chapter), and it's even made large inroads in enterprises as well.

If you haven't come across Docker before, here's a quick explanation: it's modeled on the idea of shipping containers. You specify a bundle of files (typically, using a Dockerfile) that Docker uses to build an *image*, and Docker then runs that image in a *container*, which is an isolated process on your system that can see only the files you've specified and the programs you've told it to run. You can then share the Dockerfile so people can build their own images, but a more common approach is to push the created image to a *registry*, which is a list of Docker images that can be downloaded by anybody with access. These registries can be public or private; the Docker corporation runs Docker Hub (*https://hub.docker.com*), which is a public registry that contains over 100,000 Docker images, but many companies run private registries for internal use.

What we need to do is write our own Dockerfile. This might sound a little overwhelming. What do we have to tell Docker to install? Our code? PyTorch? Conda? Python? Linux itself? Thankfully, Dockerfiles can inherit from other images, so we could, for example, inherit from the standard Ubuntu image and install Python,

PyTorch, and everything else from there. But we can do better! A selection of Conda images is available to choose from that will give us a base Linux, Python, and Anaconda installation to build on. Here's an example Dockerfile that can be used to build a container image for our service:

```
FROM continuumio/miniconda3:latest

ARG model_parameter_location
ARG model_parameter_name
ARG port
ARG host

ENV CATFISH_PORT=$port
ENV CATFISH_HOST=$host
ENV CATFISH_MODEL_LOCATION=/app/$model_parameter_name

RUN conda install -y flask \
    && conda install -c pytorch  torchvision \
    && conda install waitress
RUN mkdir -p /app

COPY ./model.py /app
COPY ./server.py /app
COPY $model_location/$model_weights_name /app/
COPY ./run-model-service.sh /

EXPOSE $port

ENTRYPOINT ["/run-model-service.sh"]
```

A few things are happening here, so let's take a look. The first line in almost all Dockerfiles will be FROM, which lists the Docker image that this file inherits from. In this case, it's continuumio/miniconda3:latest. The first part of this string is the image name. Images are also versioned, so everything after the colon is a *tag* indicating which version of the image we want to download. There's also a magic tag latest, which we use here to download the latest version of the image we're after. You may want to pin your service to a particular version so you aren't surprised by possible later changes in the base image causing issues in yours.

ARG and ENV deal with variables. ARG specifies a variable that is supplied to Docker when we're building the image, and then the variable can be used later in the Dockerfile. ENV allows you to specify environment variables that will be injected into the container at runtime. In our container, we use ARG to specify, for example, that port is a configurable option, and then use ENV to ensure that the configuration is available to our script at startup.

Having done that, RUN and COPY allow us to manipulate the image we've inherited from. RUN runs actual commands within the image, and any changes are saved as a new *layer* of the image on top of the base layer. COPY takes something from the Docker build context (typically, any files from the directory that the build command has issued or any subdirectories) and inserts it into a location on the image's filesystem. Having created /app by using RUN, we then use COPY to move our code and model parameters into the image.

EXPOSE indicates to Docker which port should be mapped to the outside world. By default, no ports are opened, so we add one here, taken from the ARG command earlier in the file. Finally, ENTRYPOINT is the default command that is run when a container is created. Here we've specified a script, but we haven't made it yet! Let's do that before we build our Docker image:

```
#!/bin/bash
#run-model-service.sh
cd /app
waitress-serve --call 'catfish_server:create_app'
```

Wait, what's happening here? Where did waitress come from? The issue is that when we were running our Flask-based server before it used a simple web server that is meant only for debugging purposes. If we want to put this into production, we need a production-grade web server. Waitress fulfills that requirement. We don't need to go into much detail about it, but you can check out the Waitress documentation (*https://oreil.ly/x96lr*) if you want to learn more.

With all that set up, we can finally create our image by using docker build:

```
docker build -t catfish-service .
```

We can make sure that the image is available on our system by using docker images:

```
>docker images
REPOSITORY          TAG          IMAGE ID
catfish-service     latest       e5de5ad808b6
```

Running our model prediction service can then be done using docker run:

```
docker run catfish-service -p 5000:5000
```

We also use the -p argument to map the container's port 5000 to our computer's port 5000. You should be able to go back to *http://localhost:5000/predict* just as before.

One thing you might notice when running docker images locally is that our Docker image is over 4GB in size! That's quite big, considering we didn't write much code. Let's look at ways to make that image smaller and make our image more practical for deployment at the same time.

Local Versus Cloud Storage

Obviously, the easiest answer to where to store our saved model parameters is on the local filesystem, whether that's on our computer or the filesystem within a Docker container. But there are a couple of problems with this. First, the model is hardcoded into the image. Also, it's quite possible that after the image is built and put into production, we need to update the model. With our current Dockerfile, we have to completely rebuild the image, even if the model's structure hasn't changed! Second, most of the size of our images comes from the size of the parameter file. You may not have noticed that they tend to be quite large! Try this out for size:

```
ls -l
total 641504
-rw------- 1 ian ian 178728960 Feb  4  2018 resnet101-5d3b4d8f.pth
-rw------- 1 ian ian 241530880 Feb 18  2018 resnet152-b121ed2d.pth
-rw------- 1 ian ian  46827520 Sep 10  2017 resnet18-5c106cde.pth
-rw------- 1 ian ian  87306240 Dec 23  2017 resnet34-333f7ec4.pth
-rw------- 1 ian ian 102502400 Oct  1  2017 resnet50-19c8e357.pth
```

If we add these models to the filesystem on every build, our Docker images will likely be quite large, which makes pushing and pulling slower. What I suggest is local filesystems or Docker volume-mapped containers if you're running on-premises, but if you're doing a cloud deployment, which we are leading up to, it makes sense to take advantage of the cloud. Model parameter files can be uploaded to Azure Blob Storage, Amazon Simple Storage Service (Amazon S3), or Google Cloud Storage and be pulled in at startup.

We can rewrite our `load_model()` function to download the parameter file at startup:

```
from urllib.request import urlopen
from shutil import copyfileobj
from tempfile import NamedTemporaryFile


def load_model():
  m = CatfishModel()
  parameter_url = os.environ["CATFISH_MODEL_LOCATION"]
  with urlopen(url) as fsrc, NamedTemporaryFile() as fdst:
    copyfileobj(fsrc, fdst)
    m.load_state_dict(torch.load(fdst))
  return m
```

There are, of course, many ways of downloading files with Python; Flask even comes with the `requests` module that would easily download the file. A potential issue, though, is that many approaches download the entire file into memory before writing it to disk. Most of the time, that makes sense, but when downloading model parameter files, they could get into the gigabyte range. So in this new version of `load_model()`, we use `urlopen()` and `copyfileobj()` to carry out the copying, and

`NamedTemporaryFile()` to give us a destination that can be deleted at the end of the block, as by that point, we've already loaded the parameters in, and thus no longer need the file! This allows us to simplify our Dockerfile:

```
FROM continuumio/miniconda3:latest

ARG port
ARG host

ENV CATFISH_PORT=$port
RUN conda install -y flask \
   && conda install -c pytorch torch torchvision \
   && conda install waitress
RUN mkdir -p /app

COPY ./model.py /app
COPY ./server.py /app
COPY ./run-model-service.sh /

EXPOSE $port

ENTRYPOINT ["/run-model-service.sh"]
```

When we run this with `docker run`, we pass in the environment variable:

```
docker run catfish-service --env CATFISH_MODEL_LOCATION=[URL]
```

The service now pulls the parameters from the URL, and the Docker image is probably around 600MB–700MB smaller than the original one.

> In this example, we assume that the model parameter file is located at a publicly accessible location. If you are deploying a model service, you likely won't be in that situation and will instead be pulling from a cloud storage layer like Amazon S3, Google Cloud Storage, or Azure Blob Storage. You'll have to use the respective provider's APIs to download the file and obtain credentials to gain access to it, both of which we don't discuss here.

We now have a model service that's capable of talking over HTTP with JSON. Now we need to make sure that we can monitor it while it makes predictions.

Logging and Telemetry

One thing that we don't have in our current service is any concept of logging. And although the service is incredibly simple and perhaps doesn't need copious logging (except in the case of catching our error states), it would be useful, if not essential, for us to keep track of what's actually being predicted. At some point, we're going to want to evaluate the model; how can we do that without production data?

Let's assume that we have a method `send_to_log()` that takes a Python `dict` and sends it elsewhere (perhaps, say, into an Apache Kafka cluster that backs up onto cloud storage). We could send appropriate information through this method every time we make a prediction:

```python
import uuid
import logging
logging.basicConfig(level=logging.INFO)

def predict():
  img_url = request.image_url
  img_tensor = open_image(BytesIO(response.content))
  start_time = time.process_time()
  prediction = model(img_tensor)
  end_time = time.process_time()
  predicted_class = CatfishClasses[torch.argmax(prediction)]
  send_to_log(
    {"image": img_url,
    "prediction": predicted_class},
    "predict_tensor": prediction,
    "img_tensor": img_tensor,
    "predict_time": end_time-start_time,
    "uuid":uuid.uuid4()
    })
  return jsonify({"image": img_url, "prediction": predicted_class})

def send_to_log(log_line):
  logger.info(log_line)
```

With a few additions to calculate how long a prediction takes, on every request, this method now sends off a message to a logger or an external resource, providing important details such as the image URL, the predicted class, the actual prediction tensor, and even the complete image tensor just in case the supplied URL is transient. We also include a generated universally unique identifier (UUID), so that this prediction can always be uniquely referenced at a later time, perhaps if its predicted class needs to be corrected. In an actual deployment, you'd include things like `user_ids` and such so that downstream systems can provide a facility for users to indicate whether the prediction was correct or incorrect, sneakily generating more training data for further training iterations of the model.

And with that, we're ready to deploy our container into the cloud. Let's take a quick look at using Kubernetes to host and scale our service.

Deploying on Kubernetes

It's beyond the scope of this book to go too deeply into Kubernetes, so we'll stick to the basics, including how to get a service quickly up and running.[1] *Kubernetes* (also known as *k8s*) is rapidly becoming the major cluster framework in the cloud. Born from Google's original cluster management software, Borg, it contains all the parts and glue to form a resilient and reliable way of running services, including things like load balancers, resource quotas, scaling policies, traffic management, sharing secrets, and more.

You can download and set up Kubernetes on your local machine or in your cloud account, but the recommended way is to use a hosted service where management of Kubernetes itself is handled by the cloud provider and you're just left with scheduling your services. We use the Google Kubernetes Engine (GKE) service for our deployment, but you could also deploy on Amazon, Azure, or DigitalOcean.

Setting Up on Google Kubernetes Engine

To use GKE, you need a Google Cloud account (*https://cloud.google.com*). In addition, running services on GKE isn't free. On the bright side, if you're new to Google Cloud, you'll get $300 in free credit, and we're probably not going to burn more than a dollar or two.

Once you have an account, download the gcloud SDK (*https://cloud.google.com/sdk*) for your system. Once that's installed, we can use it to install kubectl, the application that we'll use to interact with the Kubernetes cluster we'll be creating:

```
gcloud login
gcloud components install kubectl
```

We then need to create a new *project*, which is how Google Cloud organizes compute resources in your account:

```
gcloud projects create ml-k8s --set-as-default
```

Next, we rebuild our Docker image and tag it so it can be pushed up to the internal registry that Google provides (we need to use gcloud to authenticate), and then we can use docker push to send our container image up to the cloud. Note that we're also tagging our service with a v1 version tag, which we weren't doing before:

```
docker build -t gcr.io/ml-k8s/catfish-service:v1 .
gcloud auth configure-docker
docker push gcr.io/ml-k8s/catfish-service:v1
```

---

[1] *Cloud Native DevOps with Kubernetes* (*https://oreil.ly/2BaE1iq*) by John Arundel and Justin Domingus (O'Reilly) is a great deep dive into this framework.

Creating a k8s Cluster

Now we can create our Kubernetes cluster. In the following command, we're creating one with two n1-standard-1 nodes, Google's cheapest and lowest-powered instances. If you're really saving pennies, you can create the cluster with just one node.

```
gcloud container clusters create ml-cluster --num-nodes=2
```

This may take a couple of minutes to fully initialize the new cluster. Once it's ready, we can use kubectl to deploy our application!

```
kubectl run catfish-service
--image=gcr.io/ml-k8s/catfish-service:v1
--port 5000
--env CATFISH_MODEL_LOCATION=[URL]
```

Note that we're passing the location of the model parameter file as an environment parameter here, just as we did with the docker run command on our local machine. Use kubectl get pods to see what pods are running on the cluster. A *pod* is a group of one or more containers combined with a specification on how to run and manage those containers. For our purposes, we run our model in one container in one pod. Here's what you should see:

```
NAME                                    READY STATUS  RESTARTS  AGE
gcr.io/ml-k8s/catfish-service:v1        1/1   Running 0 4m15s
```

Right, so now we can see that our application is running, but how do we actually talk to it? To do that, we need to deploy a *service*, in this case a load balancer that maps an external IP address to our internal cluster:

```
kubectl expose deployment catfish-service
--type=LoadBalancer
--port 80
--target-port 5000
```

You can then look at the running services by using kubectl get services to get the external IP:

```
kubectl get service

NAME            CLUSTER-IP     EXTERNAL-IP    PORT(S)       AGE
catfish-service 10.3.251.122   203.0.113.0    80:30877/TCP  3d
```

You should now be able to hit *http://external-ip/predict* just as you could on your local machine. Success! We can also check in on our pod's logs without logging into it:

```
kubectl logs catfish-service-xxdsd
>> log response
```

We now have a deployment running in a Kubernetes cluster. Let's explore some of the power that it provides.

Scaling Services

Say we decide that one pod isn't enough to handle all the traffic coming into our prediction service. In a traditional deployment, we'd have to bring up new servers, add them into load balancers, and work out what to do if one of the servers fails. But with Kubernetes, we can do all this easily. Let's make sure that three copies of the service are running:

```
kubectl scale deployment hello-web --replicas=3
```

If you keep looking at `kubectl get pods`, you'll soon see that Kubernetes is bringing up two more pods from your Docker image and wiring them into the load balancer. Even better, let's see what happens if we delete one of the pods:

```
kubectl delete pod [PODNAME]
kubectl get pods
```

You'll see that the pod we've specified has been deleted. But—you should also see that a new pod is being spun up to replace it! We've told Kubernetes that we should be running three copies of the image, and because we deleted one, the cluster starts up a new pod to ensure that the replica count is what we requested. This also carries over to updating our application, so let's look at that too.

Updates and Cleaning Up

When it comes to pushing an update to our service code, we create a new version of the container with a v2 tag:

```
docker build -t gcr.io/ml-k8s/catfish-service:v2 .
docker push gcr.io/ml-k8s/catfish-service:v2
```

Then we tell the cluster to use the new image for the deployment:

```
kubectl set image deployment/catfish-service
    catfish-service=gcr.io/ml-k8s/catfish-service:v2
```

Keep monitoring via `kubectl get pods` and you'll see that new pods with the new image are being rolled out, and the pods with the old image are being deleted. Kubernetes automatically takes care of draining connections and removing the old pods from the load balancer.

Finally, if you're finished playing around with the cluster, you should clean up so you don't get any further surprise charges:

```
kubectl delete service catfish-service
gcloud container clusters delete ml-k8s
```

That wraps up our mini-tour of Kubernetes; you now know just enough to be dangerous, but definitely check out the Kubernetes website (*https://kubernetes.io*) as a starting point for further information about the system (and trust me, there's a lot of it!)

We've covered how to deploy our Python-based code, but perhaps surprisingly, PyTorch isn't limited to just Python. In the next section, you'll see how TorchScript brings in the wider world of C++, as well as some optimizations to our normal Python models.

TorchScript

If you can remember as far back as the introduction (I know!), you know that the main difference between PyTorch and TensorFlow is that TensorfFlow has a graph-based representation of a model, whereas PyTorch has an eager execution with tape-based differentiation. The eager method allows you to do all sorts of dynamic approaches to specifying and training models that makes PyTorch appealing for research purposes. On the other hand, the graph-based representation may be static, but it gains power from that stability; optimizations may be applied to the graph representation, safe in the knowledge that nothing is going to change. And just as TensorFlow has moved to support eager execution in version 2.0, version 1.0 of PyTorch introduced TorchScript, which is a way of bringing the advantages of graph-based systems without completely giving up the flexibility of PyTorch. This is done in two ways that can be mixed and matched: tracing and using TorchScript directly.

Tracing

PyTorch 1.0 comes with a JIT tracing engine that will turn an existing PyTorch module or function into a TorchScript one. It does this by passing an example tensor through the module and returning a `ScriptModule` result that contains the TorchScript representation of the original code.

Let's have a look at tracing AlexNet:

```
model = torchvision.models.AlexNet()
traced_model = torch.jit.trace(model,
                torch.rand(1, 3, 224, 224))
```

Now, this will *work*, but you'll get a message like this from the Python interpreter that will make you pause:

```
TracerWarning: Trace had nondeterministic nodes. Nodes:
%input.15 :
Float(1, 9216) = aten::dropout(%input.14, %174, %175),
scope: AlexNet/Sequential[classifier]/Dropout[0]
%input.18 :
Float(1, 4096) = aten::dropout(%input.17, %184, %185),
scope: AlexNet/Sequential[classifier]/Dropout[3]

This may cause errors in trace checking.
To disable trace checking, pass check_trace=False to torch.jit.trace()

_check_trace([example_inputs], func, executor_options,
```

```
module, check_tolerance, _force_outplace)
/home/ian/anaconda3/lib/
python3.6/site-packages/torch/jit/__init__.py:642:
TracerWarning: Output nr 1. of the traced function does not
match the corresponding output of the Python function. Detailed error:

Not within tolerance rtol=1e-05 atol=1e-05 at input[0, 22]
(0.010976361110806465 vs. -0.005604125093668699)
and 996 other locations (99.00%)
_check_trace([example_inputs], func,
executor_options, module, check_tolerance
_force_outplace)
```

What's going on here? When we create AlexNet (or other models), the model is instantiated in *training* mode. During training in many models such as AlexNet, we use a Dropout layer that randomly kills activations as a tensor goes through a network. What the JIT has done is send the random tensor we've generated through the model twice, compared them, and noted that the Dropout layers don't match. This reveals an important caveat with the tracing facility; it cannot cope with nondeterminism or control flow. If your model uses these features, you'll have to use Torch-Script directly for at least part of your conversion.

In AlexNet's case, though, the fix is simple: we'll switch the model to evaluation mode by using model.eval(). If you run the tracing line again, you'll find that it completes without any complaining. We can also print() the traced model to see what it is composed of:

```
print(traced_model)

TracedModule[AlexNet](
(features): TracedModule[Sequential](
  (0): TracedModule[Conv2d]()
  (1): TracedModule[ReLU]()
  (2): TracedModule[MaxPool2d]()
  (3): TracedModule[Conv2d]()
  (4): TracedModule[ReLU]()
  (5): TracedModule[MaxPool2d]()
  (6): TracedModule[Conv2d]()
  (7): TracedModule[ReLU]()
  (8): TracedModule[Conv2d]()
  (9): TracedModule[ReLU]()
  (10): TracedModule[Conv2d]()
  (11): TracedModule[ReLU]()
  (12): TracedModule[MaxPool2d]()
)
(classifier): TracedModule[Sequential](
  (0): TracedModule[Dropout]()
  (1): TracedModule[Linear]()
  (2): TracedModule[ReLU]()
  (3): TracedModule[Dropout]()
  (4): TracedModule[Linear]()
```

```
    (5): TracedModule[ReLU]()
    (6): TracedModule[Linear]()
    )
  )
```

We can also see the code that the JIT engine has created if we call print(traced_model.code):

```
def forward(self,
  input_1: Tensor) -> Tensor:
  input_2 = torch._convolution(input_1, getattr(self.features, "0").weight,
  getattr(self.features, "0").bias,
  [4, 4], [2, 2], [1, 1], False, [0, 0], 1, False, False, True)
  input_3 = torch.threshold_(input_2, 0., 0.)
  input_4, _0 = torch.max_pool2d_with_indices
  (input_3, [3, 3], [2, 2], [0, 0], [1, 1], False)
  input_5 = torch._convolution(input_4, getattr
  (self.features, "3").weight, getattr(self.features, "3").bias,
  [1, 1], [2, 2], [1, 1], False, [0, 0], 1, False, False, True)
  input_6 = torch.threshold_(input_5, 0., 0.)
  input_7, _1 = torch.max_pool2d_with_indices
  (input_6, [3, 3], [2, 2], [0, 0], [1, 1], False)
  input_8 = torch._convolution(input_7, getattr(self.features, "6").weight,
  getattr
  (self.features, "6").bias,
  [1, 1], [1, 1], [1, 1], False, [0, 0], 1, False, False, True)
  input_9 = torch.threshold_(input_8, 0., 0.)
  input_10 = torch._convolution(input_9, getattr
  (self.features, "8").weight, getattr(self.features, "8").bias,
  [1, 1], [1, 1], [1, 1], False, [0, 0], 1, False, False, True)
  input_11 = torch.threshold_(input_10, 0., 0.)
  input_12 = torch._convolution(input_11, getattr
  (self.features, "10").weight, getattr(self.features, "10").bias,
  [1, 1], [1, 1], [1, 1], False, [0, 0], 1, False, False, True)
  input_13 = torch.threshold_(input_12, 0., 0.)
  x, _2 = torch.max_pool2d_with_indices
  (input_13, [3, 3], [2, 2], [0, 0], [1, 1], False)
  _3 = ops.prim.NumToTensor(torch.size(x, 0))
  input_14 = torch.view(x, [int(_3), 9216])
  input_15 = torch.dropout(input_14, 0.5, False)
  _4 = torch.t(getattr(self.classifier, "1").weight)
  input_16 = torch.addmm(getattr(self.classifier, "1").bias,
    input_15, _4, beta=1, alpha=1)
  input_17 = torch.threshold_(input_16, 0., 0.)
  input_18 = torch.dropout(input_17, 0.5, False)
  _5 = torch.t(getattr(self.classifier, "4").weight)
  input_19 = torch.addmm(getattr(self.classifier, "4").bias,
    input_18, _5, beta=1, alpha=1)
  input = torch.threshold_(input_19, 0., 0.)
  _6 = torch.t(getattr(self.classifier, "6").weight)
  _7 = torch.addmm(getattr(self.classifier, "6").bias, input,
    _6, beta=1, alpha=1)
  return _7
```

The model (code and parameters) can then be saved with `torch.jit.save`:

```
torch.jit.save(traced_model, "traced_model")
```

That covers how tracing works. Let's see how to use TorchScript.

Scripting

You might wonder why we just can't trace everything. Although the tracer is good at what it does, it has limitations. For example, a simple function like the following is not possible to trace with a single pass:

```
import torch

def example(x, y):
  if x.min() > y.min():
      r = x
  else:
      r = y
  return r
```

A single trace through the function will take us down one pathway and not the other, meaning that the function will not be converted correctly. In these cases, we can use TorchScript, which is a limited subset of Python, and produce our compiled code. We use an *annotation* to tell PyTorch that we are using TorchScript, so the TorchScript implementation would look like this:

```
@torch.jit.script
def example(x, y):
    if x.min() > y.min():
        r = x
    else:
        r = y
    return r
```

Happily, we're not using any constructs in our function that aren't in TorchScript or referencing any global state, so this will just work. If we were creating a new architecture, we'd need to inherit from `torch.jit.ScriptModule` instead of `nn.Module`. You might wonder how we can use other modules (say, CNN-based layers) if all modules have to inherit from this different class. Is everything slightly different? The fix is that we can mix and match both by using explicit TorchScript and traced objects at will.

Let's go back to our CNNNet/AlexNet structure from Chapter 3 and see how it can be converted into TorchScript using a combination of these methods. For the sake of brevity, we'll implement only the `features` component:

```
class FeaturesCNNNet(torch.jit.ScriptModule):
    def __init__(self, num_classes=2):
        super(FeaturesCNNNet, self).__init__()
        self.features = torch.jit.trace(nn.Sequential(
            nn.Conv2d(3, 64, kernel_size=11, stride=4, padding=2),
```

```
        nn.ReLU(),
        nn.MaxPool2d(kernel_size=3, stride=2),
        nn.Conv2d(64, 192, kernel_size=5, padding=2),
        nn.ReLU(),
        nn.MaxPool2d(kernel_size=3, stride=2),
        nn.Conv2d(192, 384, kernel_size=3, padding=1),
        nn.ReLU(),
        nn.Conv2d(384, 256, kernel_size=3, padding=1),
        nn.ReLU(),
        nn.Conv2d(256, 256, kernel_size=3, padding=1),
        nn.ReLU(),
        nn.MaxPool2d(kernel_size=3, stride=2)
    ), torch.rand(1,3,224,224))

@torch.jit.script_method
def forward(self, x):
    x = self.features(x)
    return x
```

There are two things to note here. First, inside classes, we need to annotate using
@torch.jit.script_method. Second, although we could have traced each separate
layer individually, we took advantage of the nn.Sequential wrapper layer to fire the
trace through just that instead. You could implement the classifier block yourself
to get a feel for how this mixing works. Remember that you'll need to switch the Drop
out layers into eval() mode instead of training, and your input trace tensor will need
to be of shape [1, 256, 6, 6] because of the downsampling that the features block
carries out. And yes, you can save this network by using torch.jit.save just as we
did for the traced module. Let's have a look at what TorchScript allows and forbids.

TorchScript Limitations

The biggest restriction in TorchScript compared to Python, at least in my mind, is the
reduced number of types available. Table 8-1 lists what's available and what's not.

Table 8-1. Available Python types in TorchScript

Type	Description
tensor	A PyTorch tensor of any dtype, dimension, or backend
tuple[T0, T1,...]	A tuple containing subtypes T0, T1, etc. (e.g., tuple[tensor, tensor])
boolean	Boolean
str	String
int	Int
float	Float
list	List of type T
optional[T]	Either *None* or type T
dict[K, V]	dict with keys of type K and values of type V; K can be only str, int, or float

Another thing you can't do that you can do in standard Python is have a function that mixes return types. The following is illegal in TorchScript:

```
def maybe_a_string_or_int(x):
  if x > 3:
    return "bigger than 3!"
  else
    return 2
```

Of course, it's not really a good idea in Python, either, but the language's dynamic typing will allow it. TorchScript is statically typed (which helps with applying optimizations), so you simply can't do this in TorchScript annotated code. Also, TorchScript assumes that every parameter passed into a function is a tensor, which can result in some weirdness if you're not aware of what's going on:

```
@torch.jit.script
def add_int(x,y):
  return x + y

print(add_int.code)
>> def forward(self,
  x: Tensor,
  y: Tensor) -> Tensor:
  return torch.add(x, y, alpha=1)
```

To force different types, we need to use Python 3's type decorators:

```
@torch.jit.script
def add_int(x: int, y: int) -> int:
  return x + y
print(add_int.code)
>> def forward(self,
  x: int,
  y: int) -> int:
return torch.add(x, y)
```

As you've already seen, classes are supported, but there are a few twists. All methods on a class have to be valid TorchScript, but although this code looks valid, it will fail:

```
@torch.jit.script
class BadClass:
  def __init__(self, x)
    self.x = x

  def set_y(y)
    self.y = y
```

This is, again, a consequence of TorchScript's static typing. All instance variables have to be declared during the __init__ and cannot be introduced elsewhere. Oh, and don't get any ideas about including any expressions inside a class that aren't in a method—these are explicitly banned by TorchScript.

A useful feature of TorchScript being a subset of Python is that translation can be approached in a piecemeal approach, and the intermediate code is still valid and executable Python. TorchScript-compliant code can call out to noncompliant code, and while you won't be able to execute `torch.jit.save()` until all the noncompliant code is converted, you can still run everything under Python.

These are what I consider the major nuances of TorchScript. You can read about more in the PyTorch documentation (*https://oreil.ly/sS0o7*), which goes into depth about things like scoping (mostly standard Pythonic rules), but the outline presented here is enough to convert all the models you've seen so far in this book. Instead of regurgitating all of the reference, let's look at using one of our TorchScript-enabled models in C++.

Working with libTorch

In addition to TorchScript, PyTorch 1.0 introduced `libTorch`, a C++ library for interacting with PyTorch. Various levels of C++ interaction are available. The lowest levels are `ATen` and `autograd`, the C++ implementations of the tensor and automatic differentiation that PyTorch itself is built on. On top of those are a C++ frontend, which duplicates the Pythonic PyTorch API in C++, an interface to TorchScript, and finally an extension interface that allows new custom C++/CUDA operators to be defined and exposed to PyTorch's Python implementation. We're concerned with only the C++ frontend and the interface to TorchScript in this book, but more information on the other parts is available in the PyTorch documentation (*https://oreil.ly/y6NP5*). Let's start by getting `libTorch`.

Obtaining libTorch and Hello World

Before we can do anything, we need a C++ compiler and a way of building C++ programs on our machine. This is one of the few parts of the book where something like Google Colab isn't appropriate, so you may have to create a VM in Google Cloud, AWS, or Azure if you don't have easy access to a terminal window. (Everybody who ignored my advice not to build a dedicated machine is feeling smug right now, I bet!) The requirements for `libTorch` are a C++ compiler and *CMake*, so let's get them installed. With a Debian-based system, use this command:

```
apt install cmake g++
```

If you're using a Red Hat–based system, use this:

```
yum install cmake g++
```

Next, we need to download `libTorch` itself. To make things a little easier, for what follows, we'll use the CPU-based distribution of `libTorch`, rather than dealing with the additional CUDA dependencies that the GPU-enabled distribution brings. Create a directory called *torchscript_export* and grab the distribution:

```
wget https://download.pytorch.org/libtorch/cpu/libtorch-shared-with-deps-latest.zip
```

Use unzip to expand the ZIP file (it should create a new *libtorch* directory) and create a directory called *helloworld*. In this directory, we're going to add a minimal *CMakeLists.txt*, which *CMake* will use to build our executable:

```
cmake_minimum_required(VERSION 3.0 FATAL_ERROR)
project(helloworld)

find_package(Torch REQUIRED)

add_executable(helloworld helloworld.cpp)
target_link_libraries(helloworld "${TORCH_LIBRARIES}")
set_property(TARGET helloword PROPERTY CXX_STANDARD 11)
```

And then *helloworld.cpp* is as follows:

```
#include <torch/torch.h>
#include <iostream>

int main() {
  torch::Tensor tensor = torch::ones({2, 2});
  std::cout << tensor << std::endl;
}
```

Create a *build* directory and run **cmake**, making sure that we provide an *absolute* path to the libtorch distribution:

```
mkdir build
cd build
cmake -DCMAKE_PREFIX_PATH=/absolute/path/to/libtorch ..
cd ..
```

We can now run plain and simple make to create our executable:

```
make
./helloworld

1  1
1  1
[ Variable[CPUType]{2,2} ]
```

Congratulations on building your first C++ program with libTorch! Now, let's expand on this and see how to use the library to load in a model we've previously saved with torch.jit.save().

Importing a TorchScript Model

We're going to export our full CNNNet model from Chapter 3 and load it into C++. In Python, create an instance of the CNNNet, switch it to `eval()` mode to ignore Dropout, trace, and save to disk:

```
cnn_model = CNNNet()
cnn_model.eval()
cnn_traced = torch.jit.trace(cnn_model, torch.rand([1,3,224,224]))
torch.jit.save(cnn_traced, "cnnnet")
```

Over in the C++ world, create a new directory called *load-cnn* and add in this new *CMakeLists.txt* file:

```
cmake_minimum_required(VERSION 3.0 FATAL_ERROR)
project(load-cnn)

find_package(Torch REQUIRED)

add_executable(load-cnn.cpp load-cnn.cpp)
target_link_libraries(load-cnn "${TORCH_LIBRARIES}")
set_property(TARGET load-cnn PROPERTY CXX_STANDARD 11)
```

Let's create our C++ program, `load-cnn.cpp`:

```cpp
#include <torch/script.h>
#include <iostream>
#include <memory>

int main(int argc, const char* argv[]) {

  std::shared_ptr<torch::jit::script::Module> module = torch::jit::load("cnnnet");

  assert(module != nullptr);
  std::cout << "model loaded ok\n";

  // Create a vector of inputs.
  std::vector<torch::jit::IValue> inputs;
  inputs.push_back(torch::rand({1, 3, 224, 224}));

  at::Tensor output = module->forward(inputs).toTensor();

  std::cout << output << '\n'
}
```

A few new things are in this small program, though most of it should remind you of the Python PyTorch API. Our first act is to load in our TorchScript model with `torch::jit::load` (versus `torch.jit.load` in Python). We do a null pointer check to make sure that the model has loaded correctly, and then we move on to testing the model with a random tensor. Although we can do that fairly easily with `torch::rand`, when interacting with a TorchScript model, we have to create a vector of `torch::jit::IValue` inputs rather than just a normal tensor because of the way TorchScript is implemented in C++. Once that is done, we can push the tensor through our loaded model and then finally write the result back to standard output. We compile this in the same way that we compiled our earlier program:

```
mkdir build
cd build
cmake -DCMAKE_PREFIX_PATH=/absolute/path/to/libtorch ..
cd ..
make
./load-cnn

0.1775
0.9096
[ Variable[CPUType]{2} ]
```

And voila! A C++ program that executes a custom model with little effort on our part. Be aware that the C++ interface is still at the time of writing in beta phase, so it's possible that some of the details here may change. Make sure to have a look at the documentation before you use it in anger!

Conclusion

Hopefully you now understand how to take your trained (and debugged!) model and turn it into a Dockerized web service that can be deployed via Kubernetes. You've also seen how to use the JIT and TorchScript features to optimize our models and how to load TorchScript models in C++, giving us the promise of low-level integration of neural networks as well as in Python.

Obviously, with just one chapter, we can't cover everything about production usage of model serving. We got to the point of deploying our service, but that's not the end of the story; there's the constant monitoring of the service to make sure that it is maintaining accuracy, retraining and testing against baselines, and more complicated versioning schemes than the ones I've introduced here for both the service and the model parameters. I recommend that you log as much detail as you possibly can and take advantage of that logging information for retraining as well as monitoring purposes.

As for TorchScript, it's still early days, but a few bindings for other languages (e.g., Go and Rust) are starting to appear; by 2020 it should be easy to wire a PyTorch model into any popular language.

I've intentionally left out a few bits and pieces that don't quite line up with the book's scope. Back in the introduction, I promised that you could do everything in the book with one GPU, so we haven't talked about PyTorch's support for distributed training and inference. Also, if you read about PyTorch model exports, you're almost certainly going to come across a lot of references to the Open Neural Network Exchange

(ONNX). This standard, jointly authored by Microsoft and Facebook, was the main method of exporting models before the advent of TorchScript. Models can be exported via a similar tracing method to TorchScript and then imported in other frameworks such as Caffe2, Microsoft Cognitive Toolkit, and MXNet. ONNX is still supported and actively worked in PyTorch v1.*x*, but it appears that TorchScript is the preferred way for model exporting. See the "Further Reading" section for more details on ONNX if you're interested.

Having successfully created, debugged, and deployed our models, we'll spend the final chapter looking at what some companies have been doing with PyTorch.

Further Reading

- Flask documentation (*http://flask.pocoo.org*)
- Waitress documentation (*https://oreil.ly/bnelI*)
- Docker documentationd (*https://docs.docker.com*)
- Kubernetes (k8s) documentation (*https://oreil.ly/jMVcN*)
- TorchScript documentation (*https://oreil.ly/sS0o7*)
- Open Neural Network Exchange (*https://onnx.ai*)
- Using ONNX with PyTorch (*https://oreil.ly/UXz5S*)
- Distributed training with PyTorch (*https://oreil.ly/Q-Jao*)

CHAPTER 9

PyTorch in the Wild

For our final chapter, we'll look at how PyTorch is used by other people and companies. You'll also learn some new techniques along the way, including resizing pictures, generating text, and creating images that can fool neural networks. In a slight change from earlier chapters, we'll be concentrating on how to get up and running with existing libraries rather than starting from scratch in PyTorch. I'm hoping that this will be a springboard for further exploration.

Let's start by examining some of the latest approaches for squeezing the most out of your data.

Data Augmentation: Mixed and Smoothed

Way back in Chapter 4, we looked at various ways of augmenting data to help reduce the model overfitting on the training dataset. The ability to do more with less data is naturally an area of high activity in deep learning research, and in this section we'll look at two increasingly popular ways to squeeze every last drop of signal from your data. Both approaches will also see us changing how we calculate our loss function, so it will be a good test of the more flexible training loop that we just created.

mixup

mixup is an intriguing augmentation technique that arises from looking askew at what we want our model to do. Our normal understanding of a model is that we send it an image like the one in Figure 9-1 and want the model to return a result that the image is a fox.

Figure 9-1. A fox

But as you know, we don't get just that from the model; we get a tensor of all the possible classes and, hopefully, the element of that tensor with the highest value is the *fox* class. In fact, in the ideal scenario, we'd have a tensor that is all 0s except for a 1 in the fox class.

Except that is difficult for a neural network to do! There's always going to be uncertainty, and our activation functions like `softmax` make it difficult for the tensors to get to 1 or 0. mixup takes advantage of this by asking a question: what is the class of Figure 9-2?

Figure 9-2. A mixture of cat and fox

To our eyes, this may be a bit of a mess, but it is 60% cat and 40% fox. What if, instead of trying to make our model make a definitive guess, we could make it target two classes? This would mean that our output tensor won't run into the problem of approaching but never reaching 1 in training, and we could alter each *mixed* image by a different fraction, improving our model's ability to generalize.

But how do we calculate the loss function of this mixed-up image? Well, if p is the percentage of the first image in the mixed image, then we have a simple linear combination of the following:

```
p * loss(image1) + (1-p) * loss(image2)
```

It has to predict those images, right? And we need to scale according to how much of those images is in the final mixed image, so this new loss function seems reasonable. To choose p, we could just use random numbers drawn from a normal or uniform distribution as we would do in many other cases. However, the writers of the mixup paper determined that samples drawn from the *beta* distribution work out much better in practice.[1] Don't know what the beta distribution looks like? Well, neither did I until I saw this paper! Figure 9-3 shows how it looks when given the characteristics described in the paper.

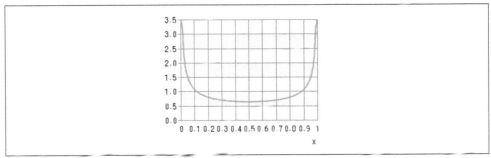

Figure 9-3. Beta distribution, where $\alpha = \beta$

The U-shape is interesting because it tells us that most of the time, our mixed image will be mainly one image or another. Again, this makes intuitive sense as we can imagine the network is going to have a harder time working out a 50/50 mixup than a 90/10 one.

Here's a modified training loop that takes a new additional data loader, `mix_loader`, and mixes the batches together:

```
def train(model, optimizer, loss_fn, train_loader, val_loader,
epochs=20, device, mix_loader):
    for epoch in range(epochs):
        model.train()
        for batch in zip(train_loader,mix_loader):
            ((inputs, targets),(inputs_mix, targets_mix)) = batch
            optimizer.zero_grad()
            inputs = inputs.to(device)
            targets = targets.to(device)
```

---

1 See "mixup: Beyond Empirical Risk Minimization" (*https://arxiv.org/abs/1710.09412*) by Hongyi Zhang et al. (2017).

```
    inputs_mix = inputs_mix.to(device)
    target_mix = targets_mix.to(device)

    distribution = torch.distributions.beta.Beta(0.5,0.5)
    beta = distribution.expand(torch.zeros(batch_size).shape).sample().to(device)

    # We need to transform the shape of beta
    # to be in the same dimensions as our input tensor
    # [batch_size, channels, height, width]

    mixup = beta[:, None, None, None]

    inputs_mixed = (mixup * inputs) + (1-mixup * inputs_mix)

    # Targets are mixed using beta as they have the same shape

    targets_mixed = (beta * targets) + (1-beta * inputs_mix)

    output_mixed = model(inputs_mixed)

    # Multiply losses by beta and 1-beta,
    # sum and get average of the two mixed losses

    loss = (loss_fn(output, targets) * beta
            + loss_fn(output, targets_mixed)
            * (1-beta)).mean()

    # Training method is as normal from herein on

    loss.backward()
    optimizer.step()
    …
```

What's happening here is after we get our two batches, we use `torch.distribu`
`tion.Beta` to generate a series of mix parameters, using the `expand` method to produce a tensor of [1, batch_size]. We could iterate through the batch and generate the parameters one by one, but this is neater, and remember, GPUs love matrix multiplication, so it'll end up being faster to do all the calculations across the batch at once (this is shown in Chapter 7 when fixing our `BadRandom` transformation, remember!). We multiply the entire batch by this tensor, and then the batch to mix in by 1 - `mix_factor_tensor` using broadcasting (which we covered in Chapter 1).

We then take the losses of the predictions against our targets for both images, and our final loss is the mean of the sum of those losses. What's happening there? Well, if you look at the source code for `CrossEntropyLoss`, you'll see the comment `The losses are averaged across observations for each minibatch`. There's also a `reduc` `tion` parameter that has a default set to `mean` (we've used the default so far, so that's why you haven't seen it before!). We need to preserve that condition, so we take the mean of our combined losses.

Now, having two data loaders isn't too much trouble, but it does make the code a little more complicated. If you run this code, you might error out because the batches are not balanced as final batches come out of the loaders, meaning that you'll have to write extra code to handle that case. The authors of the mixup paper suggest that you could replace the mix data loader with a random shuffle of the incoming batch. We can do this with `torch.randperm()`:

```
shuffle = torch.randperm(inputs.size(0))
inputs_mix = inputs[shuffle]
targets_mix = targets[shuffle]
```

When using mixup in this way, be aware that you are much more likely to get *collisions* where you end up applying the same parameter to the same set of images, potentially reducing the accuracy of training. For example, you could have cat1 mixed with fish1, and draw a beta parameter of 0.3. Then later in the same batch, you pull out fish1 and it gets mixed with cat1 with a parameter of 0.7—making it the same mix! Some implementations of mixup—in particular, the fast.ai implementation—resolve this issue by replacing our mix parameters with the following:

```
mix_parameters = torch.max(mix_parameters, 1 - mix_parameters)
```

This ensures that the nonshuffled batch will always have the highest component when being merged with the mix batch, thus eliminating that potential issue.

Oh, and one more thing: we performed the mixup transformation *after* our image transformation pipeline. At this point, our batches are just tensors that we've added together. This means that there's no reason mixup training should be restricted to images. We could use it on any type of data that's been transformed into tensors, whether text, image, audio, or anything else.

We can still do a little more to make our labels work harder for us. Enter another approach that is now a mainstay of state-of-the-art models: *label smoothing*.

Label Smoothing

In a similar manner to mixup, *label smoothing* helps to improve model performance by making the model less sure of its predictions. Instead of trying to force it to predict 1 for the predicted class (which has all the problems we talked about in the previous section), we instead alter it to predict 1 minus a small value, *epsilon*. We can create a new loss function implementation that wraps up our existing `CrossEntropyLoss` function with this functionality. As it turns out, writing a custom loss function is just another subclass of `nn.Module`:

```
class LabelSmoothingCrossEntropyLoss(nn.Module):
    def __init__(self, epsilon=0.1):
        super(LabelSmoothingCrossEntropyLoss, self).__init__()
        self.epsilon = epsilon
```

```
def forward(self, output, target):
    num_classes = output.size()[-1]
    log_preds = F.log_softmax(output, dim=-1)
    loss = (-log_preds.sum(dim=-1)).mean()
    nll = F.nll_loss(log_preds, target)
    final_loss = self.epsilon * loss / num_classes +
                 (1-self.epsilon) * nll
    return final_loss
```

When it comes to computing the loss function, we calculate the cross-entropy loss as per the implementation of `CrossEntropyLoss`. Our `final_loss` is constructed from negative log-likelihood being multiplied by 1 minus epsilon (our *smoothed* label) added to the loss multiplied by epsilon divided by the number of classes. This occurs because we are smoothing not only the label for the predicted class to be 1 minus epsilon, but also the other labels so that they're not being forced to zero, but instead a value between zero and epsilon.

This new custom loss function can replace `CrossEntropyLoss` in training anywhere we've used it in the book, and when combined with mixup, it is an incredibly effective way of getting that little bit more from your input data.

We'll now turn away from data augmentation to have a look at another hot topic in current deep learning trends: generative adversarial networks.

Computer, Enhance!

One odd consequence of the increasing power of deep learning is that for decades, we computer people have been mocking television crime shows that have a detective click a button to make a blurry camera image suddenly become a sharp, in-focus picture. How we laughed and cast derision on shows like CSI for doing this. Except we can now actually do this, at least up to a point. Here's an example of this witchcraft, on a smaller 256 × 256 image scaled to 512 × 512, in Figures 9-4 and 9-5.

Figure 9-4. Mailbox at 256 × 256 resolution

Figure 9-5. ESRGAN-enhanced mailbox at 512 × 512 resolution

The neural network learns how to *hallucinate* new details to fill in what's not there, and the effect can be impressive. But how does this work?

Introduction to Super-Resolution

Here's the first part of a very simple super-resolution model. To start, it's pretty much exactly the same as any model you've seen so far:

```python
class OurFirstSRNet(nn.Module):

    def __init__(self):
        super(OurFirstSRNet, self).__init__()
        self.features = nn.Sequential(
            nn.Conv2d(3, 64, kernel_size=8, stride=4, padding=2),
            nn.ReLU(inplace=True),
            nn.Conv2d(64, 192, kernel_size=2, padding=2),
            nn.ReLU(inplace=True),
            nn.Conv2d(192, 256, kernel_size=2, padding=2),
            nn.ReLU(inplace=True)
        )

    def forward(self, x):
        x = self.features(x)
        return x
```

If we pass a random tensor through the network, we end up with a tensor of shape [1, 256, 62, 62]; the image representation has been compressed into a much smaller vector. Let's now introduce a new layer type, torch.nn.ConvTranspose2d. You can think of this as a layer that inverts a standard Conv2d transform (with its own learnable parameters). We'll add a new nn.Sequential layer, upsample, and put in a simple list of these new layers and ReLU activation functions. In the forward() method, we pass input through that consolidated layer after the others:

```python
class OurFirstSRNet(nn.Module):
  def __init__(self):
      super(OurFirstSRNet, self).__init__()
      self.features = nn.Sequential(
          nn.Conv2d(3, 64, kernel_size=8, stride=4, padding=2),
          nn.ReLU(inplace=True),
          nn.Conv2d(64, 192, kernel_size=2, padding=2),
          nn.ReLU(inplace=True),
          nn.Conv2d(192, 256, kernel_size=2, padding=2),
          nn.ReLU(inplace=True)

      )
      self.upsample = nn.Sequential(
          nn.ConvTranspose2d(256,192,kernel_size=2, padding=2),
          nn.ReLU(inplace=True),
          nn.ConvTranspose2d(192,64,kernel_size=2, padding=2),
          nn.ReLU(inplace=True),
          nn.ConvTranspose2d(64,3, kernel_size=8, stride=4,padding=2),
          nn.ReLU(inplace=True)
      )

  def forward(self, x):
      x = self.features(x)
      x = self.upsample(x)
      return x
```

If you now test the model with a random tensor, you'll get back a tensor of exactly the same size that went in! What we've built here is known as an *autoencoder*, a type of network that rebuilds its input, usually after compressing it into a smaller dimension. That is what we've done here; the features sequential layer is an *encoder* that transforms an image into a tensor of size [1, 256, 62, 62], and the upsample layer is our *decoder* that turns it back into the original shape.

Our labels for training the image would, of course, be our input images, but that means we can't use loss functions like our fairly standard CrossEntropyLoss, because, well, we don't have classes! What we want is a loss function that tells us how different our output image is from our input image, and for that, taking the mean squared loss or mean absolute loss between the pixels of the image is a common approach.

Although calculating the loss in terms of pixels makes a lot of sense, it turns out that a lot of the most successful super-resolution networks use augmented loss functions that try to capture how much a generated image looks like the original, tolerating pixel loss for better performance in areas like texture and content loss. Some of the papers listed in "Further Reading" on page 190 go into deeper detail.

Now that gets us back to the same size input we entered, but what if we add another transposed convolution to the mix?

```
self.upsample = nn.Sequential(...
nn.ConvTranspose2d(3,3, kernel_size=2, stride=2)
nn.ReLU(inplace=True))
```

Try it! You should find that the output tensor is twice as big as the input. If we have access to a set of ground truth images at that size to act as labels, we can train the network to take in images at a size *x* and produce images for a size *2x*. In practice, we tend to perform this upsampling by scaling up twice as much as we need to and then adding a standard convolutional layer, like so:

```
self.upsample = nn.Sequential(......
nn.ConvTranspose2d(3,3, kernel_size=2, stride=2),
nn.ReLU(inplace=True),
nn.Conv2d(3,3, kernel_size=2, stride=2),
nn.ReLU(inplace=True))
```

We do this because the transposed convolution has a tendency to add jaggies and moiré patterns as it expands the image. By expanding twice and then scaling back down to our required size, we hopefully provide enough information to the network to smooth those out and make the output look more realistic.

Those are the basics behind super-resolution. Most current high-performing super-resolution networks are trained with a technique called the generative adversarial network, which has stormed the deep learning world in the past few years.

An Introduction to GANs

One of the universal problems in deep learning (or any machine learning application) is the cost of producing labeled data. In this book, we've mostly avoided the problem by using sample datasets that are all carefully labeled (even some that come prepackaged in easy training/validation/test sets!). But in the real world producing large quantities of labeled data. Indeed, techniques that you've learned a lot about so far, like transfer learning, have all been about doing more with less. But sometimes you need more, and *generative adversarial networks* (GANs) have a way to help.

GANs were introduced by Ian Goodfellow in a 2014 paper and are a novel way of providing more data to help train neural networks. And the approach is mainly "we know you love neural networks, so we added another."[2]

The Forger and the Critic

The setup of a GAN is as follows. Two neural networks are trained together. The first is the *generator*, which takes random noise from the vector space of the input tensors and produces fake data as output. The second network is the *discriminator*, which alternates between the generated fake data and real data. Its job is to look at the incoming inputs and decide whether they're real or fake. A simple conceptual diagram of a GAN is shown in Figure 9-6.

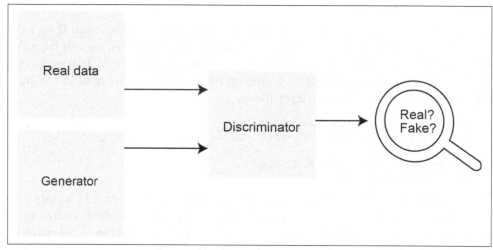

Figure 9-6. A simple GAN setup

The great thing about GANs is that although the details end up being somewhat complicated, the general idea is easy to convey: the two networks are in opposition to each other, and during training they work as hard as they can to defeat the other. By the end of the process, the *generator* should be producing data that matches the *distribution* of the real input data to flummox the *discriminator*. And once you get to that point, you can use the generator to produce more data for all your needs, while the discriminator presumably retires to the neural network bar to drown its sorrows.

---

2 See "Generative Adversarial Networks" (*https://arxiv.org/abs/1406.2661*) by Ian J. Goodfellow et al. (2014).

Training a GAN

Training a GAN is a little more complicated than training traditional networks. During the training loop, we first need to use real data to start training the discriminator. We calculate the discriminator's loss (using BCE, as we have only two classes: real or fake), and then do a backward pass to update the parameters of the discriminator as usual. But this time, we *don't* call the optimizer to update. Instead, we generate a batch of data from our generator and pass that through the model. We calculate the loss and do *another* backward pass, so at this point the training loop has calculated the losses of two passes through the model. Now, we call the optimizer to update based on these *accumulated* gradients.

In the second half of training, we turn to the generator. We give the generator access to the discriminator and then generate a new batch of data (which the generator insists is all real!) and test it against the discriminator. We form a loss against this output data, where each data point that the discriminator says is fake is considered a *wrong* answer—because we're trying to fool it—and then do a standard backward/optimize pass.

Here's a generalized implementation in PyTorch. Note that the generator and discriminator are just standard neural networks, so theoretically they could be generating images, text, audio, or whatever type of data, and be constructed of any of the types of networks you've seen so far:

```
generator = Generator()
discriminator = Discriminator()

# Set up separate optimizers for each network
generator_optimizer = ...
discriminator_optimizer = ...

def gan_train():
  for epoch in num_epochs:
    for batch in real_train_loader:
      discriminator.train()
      generator.eval()
      discriminator.zero_grad()

      preds = discriminator(batch)
      real_loss = criterion(preds, torch.ones_like(preds))
      discriminator.backward()

      fake_batch = generator(torch.rand(batch.shape))
      fake_preds = discriminator(fake_batch)
      fake_loss = criterion(fake_preds, torch.zeros_like(fake_preds))
      discriminator.backward()

      discriminator_optimizer.step()
```

```
discriminator.eval()
generator.train()
generator.zero_grad()

forged_batch = generator(torch.rand(batch.shape))
forged_preds = discriminator(forged_batch)
forged_loss = criterion(forged_preds, torch.ones_like(forged_preds))

generator.backward()
generator_optimizer.step()
```

Note that the flexibility of PyTorch helps a lot here. Without a dedicated training loop that is perhaps mainly designed for more standard training, building up a new training loop is something we're used to, and we know all the steps that we need to include. In some other frameworks, training GANs is a bit more of a fiddly process. And that's important, because training GANs is a difficult enough task without the framework getting in the way.

The Dangers of Mode Collapse

In an ideal world, what happens during training is that the discriminator will be good at detecting fakes at first, because it's training on real data, whereas the generator is allowed access to only the discriminator and not the real data itself. Eventually, the generator will learn how to fool the discriminator, and then it will soon improve rapidly to match the data distribution in order to repeatedly produce forgeries that slip past the critic.

But one thing that plagues many GAN architectures is *mode collapse*. If our real data has three types of data, then maybe our generator will start generating the first type, and perhaps it starts getting rather good at it. The discriminator may then decide that anything that looks like the first type is actually fake, even the real example itself, and the generator then starts to generate something that looks like the third type. The discriminator starts rejecting all samples of the third type, and the generator picks another one of the real examples to generate. The cycle continues endlessly; the generator never manages to settle into a period where it can generate samples from across the distribution.

Reducing mode collapse is a key performance issue of using GANs and is an ongoing research area. Some approaches include adding a similarity score to the generated data, so that potential collapse can be detected and averted, keeping a replay buffer of generated images around so that the discriminator doesn't overfit onto just the most current batch of generated images, allowing actual labels from the real dataset to be added to the generator network, and so on.

Next we round off this section by examining a GAN application that performs super-resolution.

ESRGAN

The *Enhanced Super-Resolution Generative Adversarial Network* (ESRGAN) is a network developed in 2018 that produces impressive super-resolution results. The generator is a series of convolutional network blocks with a combination of residual and dense layer connections (so a mixture of both ResNet and DenseNet), with `Batch Norm` layers removed as they appear to create artifacts in upsampled images. For the discriminator, instead of simply producing a result that says *this is real* or *this is fake*, it predicts a probability that a real image is relatively more realistic than a fake one, and this helps to make the model produce more natural results.

Running ESRGAN

To show off ESRGAN, we're going to download the code from the GitHub repository (*https://github.com/xinntao/ESRGAN*). Clone that using **git**:

```
git clone https://github.com/xinntao/ESRGAN
```

We then need to download the weights so we can use the model without training. Using the Google Drive link in the README, download the *RRDB_ESRGAN_x4.pth* file and place it in *./models*. We're going to upsample a scaled-down version of Helvetica in her box, but feel free to place any image into the *./LR* directory. Run the supplied *test.py* script and you'll see upsampled images being generated and saved into the *results* directory.

That wraps it up for super-resolution, but we haven't quite finished with images yet.

Further Adventures in Image Detection

Our image classifications in Chapters 2–4 all had one thing in common: we determined that the image belonged to a single class, cat or fish. And obviously, in real-world applications, that would be extended to a much larger set of classes. But we'd also expect images to potentially include both a cat and a fish (which might be bad news for the fish), or any of the classes we're looking for. There might be two people in the scene, a car, and a boat, and we not only want to determine that they're present in the image, but also *where* they are in the image. There are two main ways to do this: *object detection* and *segmentation*. We'll look at both and then turn to Facebook's PyTorch implementations of Faster R-CNN and Mask R-CNN to look at concrete examples.

Object Detection

Let's take a look at our cat in a box. What we really want is for the network to put the cat in a box in another box! In particular, we want a *bounding box* that encompasses everything in the image that the model thinks is *cat*, as seen in Figure 9-7.

Figure 9-7. Cat in a box in a bounding box

But how can we get our networks to work this out? Remember that these networks can predict anything that you want them to. What if alongside our prediction of a class, we also produce four more outputs? In our CATFISH model, we'd have a `Linear` layer of output size 6 instead of 2. The additional four outputs will define a rectangle using x_1, x_2, y_1, y_2 coordinates. Instead of just supplying images as training data, we'll also have to augment them with bounding boxes so that the model has something to train toward, of course. Our loss function will now be a combined loss of the cross-entropy loss of our class prediction and a mean squared loss for the bounding boxes.

There's no magic here! We just design the model to give us what we need, feed in data that has enough information to make and train to those predictions, and include a loss function that tells our network how well or badly it's doing.

An alternative to the proliferation of bounding boxes is *segmentation*. Instead of producing boxes, our network outputs an image mask of the same size of the input; the pixels in the mask are colored depending on which class they fall into. For example, grass could be green, roads could be purple, cars could be red, and so on.

As we're outputting an image, you'd be right in thinking that we'll probably end up using a similar sort of architecture as in the super-resolution section. There's a lot of cross-over between the two topics, and one model type that has become popular over the past few years is the *U-Net* architecture, shown in Figure 9-8.[3]

---

3 See "U-Net: Convolutional Networks for Biomedical Image Segmentation" (*https://arxiv.org/abs/1505.04597*) by Olaf Ronneberger et al. (2015).

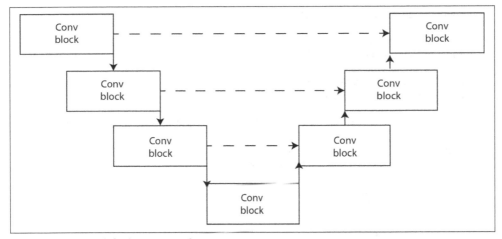

Figure 9-8. Simplified U-Net architecture

As you can see, the classic U-Net architecture is a set of convolutional blocks that scale down an image and another series of convolutions that scale it back up again to the target image. However, the key of U-Net is the lines that go across from the left blocks to their counterparts on the righthand side, which are concatenated with the output tensors as the image is scaled back up. These connections allow information from the higher level convolutional blocks to transfer across, preserving details that might be removed as the convolutional blocks reduce the input image.

You'll find U-Net-based architectures cropping up all over Kaggle segmentation competitions, proving in some ways that this structure is a good one for segmentation. Another technique that has been applied to the basic setup is our old friend transfer learning. In this approach, the first part of the U is taken from a pretrained model such as ResNet or Inception, and the other side of the U, plus skip connections, are added on top of the trained network and fine-tuned as usual.

Let's take a look at some existing pretrained models that can deliver state-of-the-art object detection and segmentation, direct from Facebook.

Faster R-CNN and Mask R-CNN

Facebook Research has produced the *maskrcnn-benchmark* library, which contains reference implementations of both object detection and segmentation algorithms. We're going to install the library and add code to generate predictions. At the time of this writing, the easiest way to build the models is by using Docker (this may change when PyTorch 1.2 is released). Clone the repository from *https://github.com/facebook research/maskrcnn-benchmark* and add this script, *predict.py*, into the *demo* directory to set up a prediction pipeline using a ResNet-101 backbone:

```
import matplotlib.pyplot as plt

from PIL import Image
import numpy as np
import sys
from maskrcnn_benchmark.config import cfg
from predictor import COCODemo

config_file = "../configs/caffe2/e2e_faster_rcnn_R_101_FPN_1x_caffe2.yaml"

cfg.merge_from_file(config_file)
cfg.merge_from_list(["MODEL.DEVICE", "cpu"])

coco_demo = COCODemo(
    cfg,
    min_image_size=500,
    confidence_threshold=0.7,
)


pil_image = Image.open(sys.argv[1])
image = np.array(pil_image)[:, :, [2, 1, 0]]
predictions = coco_demo.run_on_opencv_image(image)
predictions = predictions[:,:,::-1]

plt.imsave(sys.argv[2], predictions)
```

In this short script, we're first setting up the COCODemo predictor, making sure that we pass in the configuration that sets up Faster R-CNN instead of Mask R-CNN (which will produce segmented output). We then open an image file set on the command line, but we have to turn it into BGR format instead of RGB format as the predictor is trained on OpenCV images rather than the PIL images we've been using so far. Finally, we use imsave to write the predictions array (the original image plus bounding boxes) to a new file, also specified on the command line. Copy in a test image file into this *demo* directory and we can then build the Docker image:

```
docker build docker/
```

We run the script from inside the Docker container and produce output that looks like Figure 9-7 (I actually used the library to generate that image). Try experimenting with different confidence_threshold values and different pictures. You can also switch to the e2e_mask_rcnn_R_101_FPN_1x_caffe2.yaml configuration to try out Mask R-CNN and generate segmentation masks as well.

To train your own data on the models, you'll need to supply your own dataset that provides bounding box labels for each image. The library provides a helper function called BoxList. Here's a skeleton implementation of a dataset that you could use as a starting point:

```
from maskrcnn_benchmark.structures.bounding_box import BoxList

class MyDataset(object):
    def __init__(self, path, transforms=None):
        self.images = # set up image list
        self.boxes = # read in boxes
        self.labels = # read in labels

    def __getitem__(self, idx):
        image = # Get PIL image from self.images
        boxes = # Create a list of arrays, one per box in x1, y1, x2, y2 format
        labels = # labels that correspond to the boxes

        boxlist = BoxList(boxes, image.size, mode="xyxy")
        boxlist.add_field("labels", labels)

        if self.transforms:
            image, boxlist = self.transforms(image, boxlist)

        return image, boxlist, idx

    def get_img_info(self, idx):
        return {"height": img_height, "width": img_width
```

You'll then need to add your newly created dataset to *maskrcnn_benchmark/data/datasets/init.py* and *maskrcnn_benchmark/config/paths_catalog.py*. Training can then be carried out using the supplied *train_net.py* script in the repo. Be aware that you may have to decrease the batch size to train any of these networks on a single GPU.

That wraps it up for object detection and segmentation, though see "Further Reading" on page 190 for more ideas, including the wonderfully entitled You Only Look Once (YOLO) architecture. In the meantime, we look at how to maliciously break a model.

Adversarial Samples

You have probably seen articles online about images that can somehow prevent image recognition from working properly. If a person holds up an image to the camera, the neural network thinks it is seeing a panda or something like that. These are known as *adversarial samples*, and they're interesting ways of discovering the limitations of your architectures and how best to defend against them.

Creating an adversarial sample isn't too difficult, especially if you have access to the model. Here's a simple neural network that classifies images from the popular CIFAR-10 dataset. There's nothing special about this model, so feel free to swap it out for AlexNet, ResNet, or any other network presented so far in the book:

```
class ModelToBreak(nn.Module):
    def __init__(self):
        super(ModelToBreak, self).__init__()
        self.conv1 = nn.Conv2d(3, 6, 5)
```

```
        self.pool = nn.MaxPool2d(2, 2)
        self.conv2 = nn.Conv2d(6, 16, 5)
        self.fc1 = nn.Linear(16 * 5 * 5, 120)
        self.fc2 = nn.Linear(120, 84)
        self.fc3 = nn.Linear(84, 10)

    def forward(self, x):
        x = self.pool(F.relu(self.conv1(x)))
        x = self.pool(F.relu(self.conv2(x)))
        x = x.view(-1, 16 * 5 * 5)
        x = F.relu(self.fc1(x))
        x = F.relu(self.fc2(x))
        x = self.fc3(x)
        return x
```

Once the network has been trained on CIFAR-10, we can get a prediction for the image in Figure 9-9. Hopefully the training has gone well enough to report that it's a frog (if not, you might want to train a little more!). What we're going to do is change our picture of a frog just enough that the neural network gets confused and thinks it's something else, even though we can still recognize that it's clearly a frog.

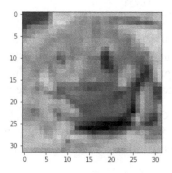

Figure 9-9. Our frog example

To do this, we'll use a method of attack called the *fast gradient sign method*.[4] The idea is to take the image we want to misclassify and run it through the model as usual, which gives us an output tensor. Typically for predictions, we'd look to see which of the tensor's values was the highest and use that as the index into our classes, using argmax(). But this time we're going to pretend that we're training the network again and backpropagate that result back through the model, giving us the gradient changes of the model with respect to the original input (in this case, our picture of a frog).

---

4 See "Explaining and Harnessing Adversarial Examples" (*https://arxiv.org/abs/1412.6572*) by Ian Goodfellow et al. (2014).

Having done that, we create a new tensor that looks at these gradients and replaces an entry with +1 if the gradient is positive and −1 if the gradient is negative. That gives us the direction of travel that this image is pushing the model's decision boundaries. We then multiply by a small scalar (called *epsilon* in the paper) to produce our malicious mask, which we then add to the original image, creating an adversarial example.

Here's a simple PyTorch method that returns the fast gradient sign tensors for an input batch when supplied with the batch's labels, plus the model and the loss function used to evaluate the model:

```
def fgsm(input_tensor, labels, epsilon=0.02, loss_function, model):
    outputs = model(input_tensor)
    loss = loss_function(outputs, labels)
    loss.backward(retain_graph=True)
    fsgm = torch.sign(inputs.grad) * epsilon
    return fgsm
```

Epsilon is normally found via experimentation. By playing around with various images, I discovered that 0.02 works well for this model, but you could also use something like a grid or random search to find the value that turns a frog into a ship!

Running this function on our frog and our model, we get a mask, which we can then add to our original image to generate our adversarial sample. Have a look at Figure 9-10 to see what it looks like!

```
model_to_break = # load our model to break here
adversarial_mask = fgsm(frog_image.unsqueeze(-1),
                        batch_labels,
                        loss_function,
                        model_to_break)
adversarial_image = adversarial_mask.squeeze(0) + frog_image
```

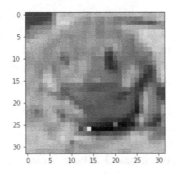

Figure 9-10. Our adversarial frog

Clearly, our created image is still a frog to our human eyes. (If it doesn't look like a frog to you, then you may be a neural network. Report yourself for a Voight-Kampff test immediately.) But what happens if we get a prediction from the model on this new image?

```
model_to_break(adversarial_image.unsqueeze(-1))
# look up in labels via argmax()
>> 'cat'
```

We have defeated the model. But is this as much of a problem as it first appears?

Black-Box Attacks

You may have noticed that to produce an image that fools the classifier, we need to know a lot about the model being used. We have the entire structure of the model in front of us as well as the loss function that was used in training the model, and we need to do forward and backward passes in the model to get our gradients. This is a classic example of what's known in computer security as a *white-box attack*, where we can peek into any part of our code to work out what's going on and exploit whatever we can find.

So does this matter? After all, most models that you'll encounter online won't allow you to peek inside. Is a *black-box attack*, where all you have is the input and output, actually possible? Well, sadly, yes. Consider that we have a set of inputs, and a set of outputs to match them against. The outputs are *labels*, and it is possible to use targeted queries of models to train a new model that you can use as a local proxy and carry out attacks in a white-box manner. Just as you've seen with transfer learning, the attacks on the proxy model can work effectively on the actual model. Are we doomed?

Defending Against Adversarial Attacks

How can we defend against these attacks? For something like classifying an image as a cat or a fish, it's probably not the end of the world, but for self-driving systems, cancer-detection applications, and so forth, it could literally mean the difference between life and death. Successfully defending against all types of adversarial attacks is still an area of research, but highlights so far include distilling and validation.

Distilling a model by using it to train *another* model seems to help. Using label smoothing with the new model, as outlined earlier in this chapter, also seems to help. Making the model less sure of its decisions appears to smooth out the gradients somewhat, making the gradient-based attack we've outlined in this chapter less effective.

A stronger approach is to go back to some parts of the early computer vision days. If we perform input validation on the incoming data, we can possibly prevent the adversarial image from getting to the model in the first place. In the preceding example, the generated attack image has a few pixels that are very out of place to what our eyes are expecting when we see a frog. Depending on the domain, we could have a filter that allows in only images that pass some filtering tests. You could in theory make a neural net to do that too, because then the attackers have to try to break two different models with the same image!

Now we really are done with images. But let's look at some developments in text-based networks that have occurred the past couple of years.

More Than Meets the Eye: The Transformer Architecture

Transfer learning has been a big feature in allowing image-based networks to become so effective and prevalent over the past decade, but text has been a more difficult nut to crack. In the last couple of years, though, some major steps have been taken that are beginning to unlock the potential of using transfer learning in text for all sorts of tasks, such as generation, classification, and answering questions. We've also seen a new type of architecture begin to take center stage: the *Transformer network*. These networks don't come from Cybertron, but the technique is behind the most powerful text-based networks we've seen, with OpenAI's GPT-2 model, released in 2019, showing a scarily impressive quality in its generated text, to the extent that OpenAI initially held back the larger version of the model to prevent it from being used for nefarious purposes. We look at the general theory of Transformer and then dive into how to use Hugging Face's implementations of GPT-2 and BERT.

Paying Attention

The initial step along the way to the Transformer architecture was the *attention* mechanism, which was initially introduced to RNNs to help in sequence-to-sequence applications such as translation.[5]

The issue *attention* was trying to solve was the difficulty in translating sentences such as "The cat sat on the mat and she purred." We know that *she* in that sentence refers to the cat, but it's a hard concept to get a standard RNN to understand. It may have the hidden state that we talked about in Chapter 5, but by the time we get to *she*, we already have a lot of time steps and hidden state for each step!

So what *attention* does is add an extra set of learnable weights attached to each time step that focuses the network onto a particular part of the sentence. The weights are normally pushed through a `softmax` layer to generate probabilities for each step and then the dot product of the attention weights is calculated with the previous hidden state. Figure 9-11 shows a simplified version of this with respect to our sentence.

---

5 See "Neural Machine Translation by Jointly Learning to Align and Translate" (*https://arxiv.org/abs/1409.0473*) by Dzmitry Bahdanau et al. (2014).

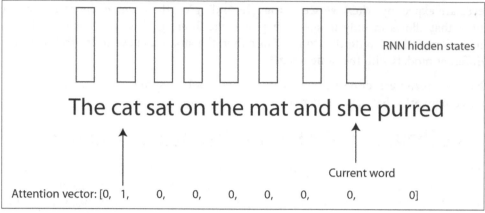

Figure 9-11. An attention vector pointing to cat

The weights ensure that when the hidden state gets combined with the current state, *cat* will be a major part of determining the output vector at the time step for *she*, which will provide useful context for translating into French, for example!

We won't go into all the details about how *attention* can work in a concrete implementation, but know the concept was powerful enough that it kickstarted the impressive growth and accuracy of Google Translate back in the mid-2010s. But more was to come.

Attention Is All You Need

In the groundbreaking paper "Attention Is All You Need,"[6] Google researchers pointed out that we'd spent all this time bolting attention onto an already slow RNN-based network (compared to CNNs or linear units, anyhow). What if we didn't need the RNN after all? The paper showed that with stacked attention-based encoders and decoders, you could create a model that didn't rely on the RNN's hidden state at all, leading the way to the larger and faster Transformer that dominates textual deep learning today.

The key idea was to use what the authors called *multihead attention*, which parallelizes the *attention* step over all the input by using a group of `Linear` layers. With these, and borrowing some residual connection tricks from ResNet, Transformer quickly began to supplant RNNs for many text-based applications. Two important Transformer releases, BERT and GPT-2, represent the current state-of-the-art as this book goes to print.

---

6 See "Attention Is All You Need" (*https://arxiv.org/abs/1706.03762*) by Ashish Vaswani et al. (2017).

Luckily for us, there's a library (*https://oreil.ly/xpDzq*) from Hugging Face that implements both of them in PyTorch. It can be installed using `pip` or `conda`, and you should also `git clone` the repo itself, as we'll be using some of the utility scripts later!

```
pip install pytorch-transformers
conda install pytorch-transformers
```

First, we'll have a look at BERT.

BERT

Google's 2018 *Bidirectional Encoder Representations from Transformers* (BERT) model was one of the first successful examples of bringing transfer learning of a powerful model to test. BERT itself is a massive Transformer-based model (weighing in at 110 million parameters in its smallest version), pretrained on Wikipedia and the Book-Corpus dataset. The issue that both Transformer and convolutional networks traditionally have when working with text is that because they see all of the data at once, it's difficult for those networks to learn the temporal structure of language. BERT gets around this in its pretraining stage by masking 15% of the text input at random and forcing the model to predict the parts that have been masked. Despite being conceptually simple, the combination of the massive size of the 340 million parameters in the largest model with the Transformer architecture resulted in new state-of-the-art results for a whole series of text-related benchmarks.

Of course, despite being created by Google with TensorFlow, there are implementations of BERT for PyTorch. Let's take a quick look at one now.

FastBERT

An easy way to start using the BERT model in your own classification applications is to use the *FastBERT* library that mixes Hugging Face's repository with the fast.ai API (which you'll see in a bit more detail when we come to ULMFiT shortly). It can be installed via `pip` in the usual manner:

```
pip install fast-bert
```

Here's a script that can be used to fine-tune BERT on our Sentiment140 Twitter dataset that we used into Chapter 5:

```
import torch
import logger

from pytorch_transformers.tokenization import BertTokenizer
from fast_bert.data import BertDataBunch
from fast_bert.learner import BertLearner
from fast_bert.metrics import accuracy

device = torch.device('cuda')
logger = logging.getLogger()
```

```
metrics = [{'name': 'accuracy', 'function': accuracy}]

tokenizer = BertTokenizer.from_pretrained
                ('bert-base-uncased',
                 do_lower_case=True)


databunch = BertDataBunch([PATH_TO_DATA],
                          [PATH_TO_LABELS],
                          tokenizer,
                          train_file=[TRAIN_CSV],
                          val_file=[VAL_CSV],
                          test_data=[TEST_CSV],
                          text_col=[TEST_FEATURE_COL], label_col=[0],
                          bs=64,
                          maxlen=140,
                          multi_gpu=False,
                          multi_label=False)


learner = BertLearner.from_pretrained_model(databunch,
                          'bert-base-uncased',
                          metrics,
                          device,
                          logger,
                          is_fp16=False,
                          multi_gpu=False,
                          multi_label=False)

learner.fit(3, lr='1e-2')
```

After our imports, we set up the `device`, `logger`, and `metrics` objects, which are required by the `BertLearner` object. We then create a `BERTTokenizer` for tokenizing our input data, and in this base we're going to use the `bert-base-uncased` model (which has 12 layers and 110 million parameters). Next, we need a `BertDataBunch` object that contains paths to the training, validation, and test datasets, where to find the label column, our batch size, and the maximum length of our input data, which in our case is simple because it can be only the length of a tweet, at that time 140 characters. Having done that, we will set up a BERT model by using the `Ber tLearner.from_pretrained_model` method. This passes in our input data, our BERT model type, the `metric`, `device`, and `logger` objects we set up at the start of the script, and finally some flags to turn off training options that we don't need but aren't given defaults for the method signature.

Finally, the `fit()` method takes care of fine-tuning the BERT model on our input data, running on its own internal training loop. In this example, we're training for three epochs with a learning rate of `1e-2`. The trained PyTorch model can be accessed afterward using `learner.model`.

And that's how to get up and running with BERT. Now, onto the competition.

GPT-2

Now, while Google was quietly working on BERT, OpenAI was working on its own version of a Transformer-based text model. Instead of using masking to force the model to learn language structure, the model constrains the attention mechanism within the architecture to simply predict the next word in a sequence, in a similar style to the RNNs in Chapter 5. As a result, GPT was somewhat left behind by the impressive performance of BERT, but in 2019 OpenAI struck back with *GPT-2*, a new version of the model that reset the bar for text generation.

The magic behind GPT-2 is scale: the model is trained on text from over 8 million websites, and the largest variant of GPT-2 weighs in at 1.5 billion parameters. And while it still doesn't dislodge BERT on particular benchmarks for things like question/answering or other NLP tasks, its ability to create incredibly realistic text from a basic prompt led to OpenAI locking the full-size model behind closed doors for fear of it being weaponized. They have, however, released smaller versions of the model, clocking in at 117 and 340 million parameters.

Here's an example of the output that GPT-2 can generate. Everything in italics was written by GPT-2's 340M model:

> Jack and Jill went up the hill *on a bike ride. The sky was a grey white and the wind was blowing, causing a heavy snowfall. It was really difficult to drive down the hill, I had to lean forward on a bit of gear to get it on. But then there was a moment of freedom that I would never forget: The bike was at a complete stop on the mountain side and I was in the middle of it. I didn't have time to say a word, but I did lean forward and touch the brakes and the bike started to go.*

Aside from switching from *Jack and Jill* to *I*, this is an impressive piece of text generation. For short pieces of text, it can sometimes be indistinguishable from human-created text. It does reveal the machine behind the curtain as the generated text continues, but it's an impressive feat that could be writing tweets and Reddit comments right now. Let's have a look at how to do this with PyTorch.

Generating Text with GPT-2

Like BERT, the official GPT-2 release from OpenAI is a TensorFlow model. Also like BERT, Hugging Face has released a PyTorch version that is contained within the same library (`pytorch-transformers`). However, a burgeoning ecosystem has been built around the original TensorFlow model that just doesn't exist currently around the PyTorch version. So just this once, we're going to cheat: we're going to use some of the TensorFlow-based libraries to fine-tune the GPT-2 model, and then export the weights and import them into the PyTorch version of the model. To save us from too much setup, we also do all the TensorFlow operations in a Colab notebook! Let's get started.

Open a new Google Colab notebook and install the library that we're using, Max Woolf's *gpt-2-simple*, which wraps up GPT-2 fine-tuning in a single package. Install it by adding this into a cell:

```
!pip3 install gpt-2-simple
```

Next up, you need some text. In this example, I'm using a public domain text of PG Wodehouse's *My Man Jeeves*. I'm also not going to do any further processing on the text after downloading it from the Project Gutenberg website with `wget`:

```
!wget http://www.gutenberg.org/cache/epub/8164/pg8164.txt
```

Now we can use the library to train. First, make sure your notebook is connected to a GPU (look in Runtime→Change Runtime Type), and then run this code in a cell:

```
import gpt_2_simple as gpt2

gpt2.download_gpt2(model_name="117M")

sess = gpt2.start_tf_sess()
gpt2.finetune(sess,
              "pg8164.txt",model_name="117M",
              steps=1000)
```

Replace the text file with whatever text file you're using. As the model trains, it will spit out a sample every hundred steps. In my case, it was interesting to see it turn from spitting out vaguely Shakespearian play scripts to something that ended up approaching Wodehouse prose. This will likely take an hour or two to train for 1,000 epochs, so go off and do something more interesting instead while the cloud's GPUs are whirring away.

Once it has finished, we need to get the weights out of Colab and into your Google Drive account so you can download them to wherever you're running PyTorch from:

```
gpt2.copy_checkpoint_to_gdrive()
```

That will point you to open a new web page to copy an authentication code into the notebook. Do that, and the weights will be tarred up and saved to your Google Drive as *run1.tar.gz*.

Now, on the instance or notebook where you're running PyTorch, download that tarfile and extract it. We need to rename a couple of files to make these weights compatible with the Hugging Face reimplementation of GPT-2:

```
mv encoder.json vocab.json
mv vocab.bpe merges.txt
```

We now need to convert the saved TensorFlow weights into ones that are compatible with PyTorch. Handily, the `pytorch-transformers` repo comes with a script to do that:

```
python [REPO_DIR]/pytorch_transformers/convert_gpt2_checkpoint_to_pytorch.py
--gpt2_checkpoint_path [SAVED_TENSORFLOW_MODEL_DIR]
--pytorch_dump_folder_path [SAVED_TENSORFLOW_MODEL_DIR]
```

Creating a new instance of the GPT-2 model can then be performed in code like this:

```
from pytorch_transformers import GPT2LMHeadModel

model = GPT2LMHeadModel.from_pretrained([SAVED_TENSORFLOW_MODEL_DIR])
```

Or, just to play around with the model, you can use the *run_gpt2.py* script to get a prompt where you enter text and get generated samples back from the PyTorch-based model:

```
python [REPO_DIR]/pytorch-transformers/examples/run_gpt2.py
--model_name_or_path [SAVED_TENSORFLOW_MODEL_DIR]
```

Training GPT-2 is likely to become easier in the coming months as Hugging Face incorporates a consistent API for all the models in its repo, but the TensorFlow method is the easiest to get started with right now.

BERT and GPT-2 are the most popular names in text-based learning right now, but before we wrap up, we cover the dark horse of the current state-of-the-art models: ULMFiT.

ULMFiT

In contrast to the behemoths of BERT and GPT-2, *ULMFiT* is based on a good old RNN. No Transformer in sight, just the AWD-LSTM, an architecture originally created by Stephen Merity. Trained on the WikiText-103 dataset, it has proven to be amendable to transfer learning, and despite the *old* type of architecture, has proven to be competitive with BERT and GPT-2 in the classification realm.

While ULMFiT is, at heart, just another model that can be loaded and used in PyTorch like any other, its natural home is within the fast.ai library, which sits on top of PyTorch and provides many useful abstractions for getting to grips with and being productive with deep learning quickly. To that end, we'll look at how to use ULMFiT with the fast.ai library on the Twitter dataset we used in Chapter 5.

We first use fast.ai's Data Block API to prepare our data for fine-tuning the LSTM:

```
data_lm = (TextList
           .from_csv("./twitter-data/",
           'train-processed.csv', cols=5,
           vocab=data_lm.vocab)
           .split_by_rand_pct()
```

```
.label_from_df(cols=0)
.databunch())
```

This is fairly similar to the `torchtext` helpers from Chapter 5 and just produces what fast.ai calls a `databunch`, from which its models and training routines can easily grab data. Next, we create the model, but in fast.ai, this happens a little differently. We create a `learner` that we interact with to train the model instead of the model itself, though we pass that in as a parameter. We also supply a dropout value (we're using the one suggested in the fast.ai training materials):

```
learn = language_model_learner(data_lm, AWD_LSTM, drop_mult=0.3)
```

Once we have our `learner` object, we can find the optimal learning rate. This is just like what we implemented in Chapter 4, except that it's built into the library and uses an exponentially moving average to smooth out the graph, which in our implementation is pretty spiky:

```
learn.lr_find()
learn.recorder.plot()
```

From the plot in Figure 9-12, it looks like `1e-2` is where we're starting to hit a steep decline, so we'll pick that as our learning rate. Fast.ai uses a method called `fit_one_cycle`, which uses a 1cycle learning scheduler (see "Further Reading" on page 190 for more details on 1cycle) and very high learning rates to train a model in an order of magnitude fewer epochs.

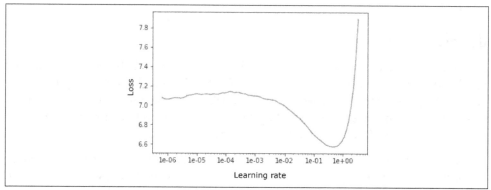

Figure 9-12. ULMFiT learning rate plot

Here, we're training for just one cycle and saving the fine-tuned head of the network (the *encoder*):

```
learn.fit_one_cycle(1, 1e-2)
learn.save_encoder('twitter_encoder')
```

With the fine-tuning of the language model completed (you may want to experiment with more cycles in training), we build a new `databunch` for the actual classification problem:

```
twitter_classifier_bunch = TextList
            .from_csv("./twitter-data/",
            'train-processed.csv', cols=5,
            vocab=data_lm.vocab)
            .split_by_rand_pct()
            .label_from_df(cols=0)
            .databunch())
```

The only real difference here is that we supply the actual labels by using `label_from_df` and we pass in a `vocab` object from the language model training that we performed earlier to make sure they're using the same mapping of words to numbers, and then we're ready to create a new `text_classifier_learner`, where the library does all the model creation for you behind the scenes. We load the fine-tuned encoder onto this new model and begin the process of training again:

```
learn = text_classifier_learner(data_clas, drop_mult=0.5)
learn.load_encoder('fine_tuned_enc')

learn.lr_find()
learn.recorder.plot()

learn.fit_one_cycle(1, 2e-2, moms=(0.8,0.7))
```

And with a tiny amount of code, we have a classifier that reports an accuracy of 76%. We could easily improve that by training the language model for more cycles, adding differential learning rates and freezing parts of the model while training, all of which fast.ai supports with methods defined on the `learner`.

What to Use?

Given that little whirlwind tour of the current cutting edge of text models in deep learning, there's probably one question on your mind: "That's all great, but which one should I actually *use*?" In general, if you're working on a classification problem, I suggest you start with ULMFiT. BERT is impressive, but ULMFiT is competitive with BERT in terms of accuracy, and it has the additional benefit that you don't need to buy a huge number of TPU credits to get the best out of it. A single GPU fine-tuning ULMFiT is likely to be enough for most people.

And as for GPT-2, if you're after generated text, then yes, it's a better fit, but for classification purposes, it's going to be harder to approach ULMFiT or BERT performance. One thing that I do think might be interesting is to let GPT-2 loose on data augmentation; if you have a dataset like Sentiment140, which we've been using throughout this book, why not fine-tune a GPT-2 model on that input and use it to generate more data?

Conclusion

This chapter looked at the wider world of PyTorch, including libraries with existing models that you can import into your own projects, some cutting-edge data augmentation approaches that can be applied to any domain, as well as adversarial samples that can ruin your model's day and how to defend against them. I hope that as we come to the end of our journey, you understand how neural networks are assembled and how to get images, text, and audio to flow through them as tensors. You should be able to train them, augment data, experiment with learning rates, and even debug models when they're not going quite right. And once all that's done, you know how to package them up in Docker and get them serving requests from the wider world.

Where do we go from here? Consider having a look at the PyTorch forums and the other documentation on the website. I definitely also recommend visiting the fast.ai community even if you don't end up using the library; it's a hive of activity, filled with good ideas and people experimenting with new approaches, while also friendly to newcomers!

Keeping up with the cutting edge of deep learning is becoming harder and harder. Most papers are published on arXiv (*https://arxiv.org*), but the rate of papers being published seems to be rising at an almost exponential level; as I was typing up this conclusion, XLNet (*https://arxiv.org/abs/1906.08237*) was released, which apparently beats BERT on various tasks. It never ends! To try to help in this, I listed a few Twitter accounts here where people often recommend interesting papers. I suggest following them to get a taste of current and interesting work, and from there you can perhaps use a tool such as arXiv Sanity Preserver (*http://arxiv-sanity.com*) to drink from the firehose when you feel more comfortable diving in.

Finally, I trained a GPT-2 model on the book and it would like to say a few words:

> Deep learning *is a key driver of how we work on today's deep learning applications, and deep learning is expected to continue to expand into new fields such as image-based classification and in 2016, NVIDIA introduced the CUDA LSTM architecture. With LSTMs now becoming more popular, LSTMs were also a cheaper and easier to produce method of building for research purposes, and CUDA has proven to be a very competitive architecture in the deep learning market.*

Thankfully, you can see there's still a way to go before we authors are out of a job. But maybe you can help change that!

Further Reading

- A survey of current super-resolution techniques (*https://arxiv.org/pdf/1902.06068.pdf*)

- Ian Goodfellow's lecture on GANs (*https://www.youtube.com/watch?v=Z6rxFNMGdn0*)
- You Only Look Once (YOLO) (*https://pjreddie.com/darknet/yolo*), a family of fast object detection models with highly readable papers
- CleverHans (*https://github.com/tensorflow/cleverhans*), a library of adversarial generation techniques for TensorFlow and PyTorch
- The Illustrated Transformer (*http://jalammar.github.io/illustrated-transformer*), an in-depth voyage through the Transformer architecture

Some Twitter accounts to follow:

- *@jeremyphoward*—Cofounder of fast.ai
- *@miles_brundage*—Research scientist (policy) at OpenAI
- *@BrundageBot*—Twitter bot that generates a daily summary of interesting papers from arXiv (warning: often tweets out 50 papers a day!)
- *@pytorch*—Official PyTorch account

Index

OK, 139
one-hot encoding, 75
ones() function, 10
ONNX (Open Neural Network Exchange), 159
OpenAI, 181, 185
optim.Adam() function, 26
optimization of neural networks, 24-26
optimizer.step() function, 26
out_channels, 36
out_features, 53
overfitting, 20, 57

P

P100, 6
P2, P3, 5
p2.xlarge, 5
pad token, 81
PadTrim, 107
pandas, 77
parameters() function, 52
partial() function, 121
PCPartPicker, 3
permute() function, 13
pip, 95, 138
plt function, 55
pod, 148
pooling in CNN, 37
predict() function, 140
predictions, 176
    and ensembling, 66
    in image classification, 28
    with torchtext, 84
preprocess() function, 84
pretrained models, 44-48
    BatchNorm, 47
    choosing, 48
    examining model structure, 44-47
print() function, 120, 151
print(model) function, 47
process() function, 84
production, deploying PyTorch applications in,
    137-160
    building a flask service, 138-140
    deploying on Kubernetes, 147-150
    Docker containers, 141-143
    libTorch, 156-159
    local versus cloud storage, 144-145
    logging and telemetry, 145
    model serving, 137-146

setting up model parameters, 140
    TorchScript, 150-156
py-spy, 127, 130
Python, 121, 137
Python 2.x, 8
PyTorch (generally), 1-14
    building a custom deep learning machine,
        1-3
    cloud platforms and, 3-7
    installation, 8-10
    origins, xi
    tensors and, 10-13
PyTorch Hub, 48
pytorch-transformers, 187

R

Raina, Rajat, x
RAM, 2
random deletion, 85
random insertion, 85
random swap, 86
RandomAffine, 62
RandomApply, 64
RandomCrop, 60
RandomGrayscale, 59
RandomResizeCrop, 60
RBG color space, 63
README, 93
rectified linear unit (see ReLU)
recurrent neural networks (RNNs), 69-71, 181
Red Hat Enterprise Linux (RHEL) 7, 9
register_backward_hook() function, 120
ReLU (rectified linear unit), 22, 30, 39, 52
remove() function, 120
requires_grad() function, 52
resample, 63
reshape() function, 12
reshaping a tensor, 12
Resize(64) transform, 19
ResNet architecture, 43, 48, 101, 175
    and frequency, 104
    and learning rate, 53-56
    transfer learning with, 51-53
ResNet-152, 132
ResNet-18, 120
RHEL (Red Hat Enterprise Linux) 7, 9
RMSProp, 25
RNNs (recurrent neural networks), 69-71, 181
ROCm, 2

About the Author

Ian Pointer is a data engineer specializing in machine learning solutions (including deep learning techniques) for multiple Fortune 100 clients. Ian is currently at Lucidworks, where he works on cutting-edge NLP applications and engineering.

He immigrated to the United States from the United Kingdom in 2011 and became an American citizen in 2017.

Colophon

The bird on the cover of *Programming PyTorch for Deep Learning* is a red-headed woodpecker (*Melanerpes erythrocephalus*). Red-headed woodpeckers are native to North America's open forests and pine savannas. They migrate throughout the eastern United States and southern Canada.

Red-headed woodpeckers don't develop their striking red feathers until they become adults. The adults have a black back and tail, red head and neck, and white undersides. In contrast, the young woodpeckers have gray heads. At maturity, these woodpeckers weigh 2–3 ounces, have a 16.5-inch wingspan, and measure 7.5–9 inches long. Females can lay four to seven eggs at a time. They breed in the spring, having up to two broods per season. Males help with incubating and feeding.

Red-headed woodpeckers eat insects—which they can catch in midair—seeds, fruits, berries, and nuts. They forage in trees and on the ground with that characteristic pecking action. For the winter, red-headed woodpeckers store nuts in holes and crevices in tree bark.

Many of the animals on O'Reilly covers are endangered; all of them are important to the world.

The cover illustration is by Susan Thompson, based on a black-and-white engraving from *Pictorial Museum of Animated Nature*. The cover fonts are Gilroy Semibold and Guardian Sans. The text font is Adobe Minion Pro; the heading font is Adobe Myriad Condensed; and the code font is Dalton Maag's Ubuntu Mono.

Milton Keynes UK
Ingram Content Group UK Ltd.
UKHW012319120824
446858UK00003B/11